INTERNATIONAL COOKBOOK

CAVENDISH HOUSE

Edited by Isabel Moore

Published by
Marshall Cavendish Books Limited
58 Old Compton Street
London W1V 5PA

© Marshall Cavendish Limited 1983

First published in 1981 as
Chinese Cooking, Italian Cooking,
Mexican Cooking, German Cooking
and *Home-Style Cooking*

Filmset in Plantin by
MS Filmsetting Ltd, Frome, Somerset

Printed by L.E.G.O., Vicenza, Italy

ISBN 0 86307 090 6

CONTENTS

CHINESE COOKING

CONTENTS

SOUPS & DIM SUM

Cucumber and Pork Soup

1.2 litres/2 pints chicken stock
5 ml/1 teaspoon salt
15 ml/1 tablespoon soya sauce
225 g/½ lb pork fillet, cut into very thin strips
2 cucumbers, peeled, halved lengthways, seeded and cut into thin slices

1. Pour the stock into a saucepan and add the salt and soya sauce. Bring to the boil, then stir in the pork strips. Simmer for 10 minutes.

2. Add the cucumbers and bring back to the boil. Simmer for a further 3 minutes or until the cucumbers are translucent. Serve hot.

Serves 4

Chicken Corn Soup

45 ml/3 tablespoons oil
4 cm/1½ in piece of fresh ginger root, peeled and chopped
175 g/6 oz finely chopped cooked chicken meat
4 dried mushrooms, soaked in cold water for 45 minutes, drained and stalks removed
400 g/14 oz canned sweetcorn, drained
600 ml/1 pint chicken stock
5 ml/1 teaspoon sugar
10 ml/2 teaspoons cornflour
15 ml/1 tablespoon water

1. Heat the oil in a saucepan. Add the ginger root and stir-fry for 2 minutes. Add the chicken and stir-fry for 2 minutes.

2. Chop the mushrooms if they are large, then add to the pan with the sweetcorn, stock and sugar. Bring to the boil, stirring well, and simmer for 10 minutes.

3. Dissolve the cornflour in the water and add to the soup. Simmer, stirring, until thickened. Serve hot.

Serves 4

Egg Drop Soup

15 ml/1 tablespoon oil
1 medium onion, thinly sliced
1 cucumber, finely diced
1.75 litres/3 pints chicken stock
4 medium tomatoes, quartered
1 egg, beaten

1. Heat the oil in a saucepan. Add the onion and stir-fry for 1 minute. Add the cucumber and stir-fry for a further 1 minute.

2. Stir in the stock and bring to the boil. Simmer gently for 10 minutes.

3. Add the tomato quarters and simmer for a further 5 minutes.

4. Remove the pan from the heat and carefully stir the egg into the soup using a fork. Serve immediately.

Serves 6

Wonton Soup

450 g/1 lb minced pork or beef
30 ml/2 tablespoons soya sauce
2.5 cm/1 in piece of fresh ginger root, peeled and finely chopped
5 ml/1 teaspoon salt
5 ml/1 teaspoon grated nutmeg
275 g/10 oz chopped spinach
36 bought wonton wrappers (or see recipe overleaf)
1.75 litres/3 pints chicken stock
1 bunch watercress, chopped

1. Mix together the pork or beef, soya sauce, ginger, salt, nutmeg and spinach. Put a little of this filling just below the centre of each wonton wrapper and dampen the edges. Fold one corner of each wonton wrapper over the filling to make a triangle and pinch the edges together to seal. Pull the corners at the base of the triangles together and pinch to seal.

2. Drop the wontons into a saucepan of boiling water. Return to the boil and simmer for 5 minutes or until the wontons are tender but still firm. Drain the water from the pan and replace with the stock. Bring to the boil, then add the watercress. Serve hot.

Serves 6

(Top) Wonton soup
(Bottom) Wonton dim sum

Wonton Dim Sum

225 g/¼ lb minced pork
10 ml/2 teaspoons rice wine or pale dry sherry
10 ml/2 teaspoons soya sauce
5 ml/1 teaspoon salt
5 ml/1 teaspoon sugar
10 ml/2 teaspoons cornflour
½ head of Chinese cabbage (pak choy), chopped
3 canned water chestnuts, finely chopped
1 spring onion, finely chopped
36 bought wonton wrappers (or see recipe below)

1. Mix together the pork, rice wine or sherry, soya sauce, salt, sugar and cornflour, using your fingers to combine the ingredients thoroughly. Work in the cabbage, water chestnuts and spring onion.

2. Put a little of the filling mixture just below the centre of each wonton wrapper and dampen the edges. Fold one corner of each wonton wrapper over the filling to make a triangle and pinch the edges together to seal. Pull the corners at the base of the triangles together and pinch to seal.

3. Arrange the wontons in one layer on a heatproof plate and steam over a saucepan of boiling water for 30 minutes. Alternatively, use an ordinary steamer or a Chinese bamboo steamer. Cook in several batches, if necessary. Serve hot.

Serves 6–8

Wonton Dough

To make your own wonton, sift 225 g/½ lb of plain flour and 5 ml/1 teaspoon of salt into a bowl. Make a well in the centre and pour in 1 egg lightly beaten with 45 ml/3 tablespoons of water. Draw the dry ingredients into the liquid until incorporated and the dough comes away from the sides of the bowl. Turn out on to a floured surface and knead for 10 minutes until elastic. Roll out thinly and cut into pieces, about 5–7.5 cm/2–3 in square.

Barbecued Spareribs

1 kg/2 lb American-style spareribs, cut into individual ribs
50 ml/2 fl oz peanut oil
2 garlic cloves, crushed
1 small onion, finely chopped
4 cm/1½ in piece of fresh ginger root, peeled and finely chopped
50 ml/2 fl oz soya sauce
45 ml/3 tablespoons rice wine or pale dry sherry
15 ml/1 tablespoon sugar
150 ml/¼ pint chicken stock

1. Rub the ribs all over with salt.

2. Heat the oil in a frying pan. Add the garlic, onion and ginger and stir-fry for 1 minute. Add the ribs, reduce the heat slightly and stir-fry for 5 minutes. Remove the ribs from the pan.

3. Add the soya sauce, wine or sherry, sugar and pepper to taste to the pan and stir well. Stir in the stock and bring to the boil.

4. Return the ribs to the pan and turn to coat with the sauce. Simmer for 5 minutes, then cover the pan and continue simmering for 30 minutes, turning the ribs over once.

5. Preheat the oven to 190°C/375°F (Gas 5). Arrange the ribs in a roasting tin and spoon over any sauce remaining in the pan. Bake for 5–10 minutes or until the ribs are crisp and dry. Serve hot.

Serves 4

NOODLES, RICE & EGGS

Shrimp Chow Mein

225 g/½ lb vermicelli
oil for deep frying
30 ml/2 tablespoons peanut oil
8 dried mushrooms, soaked in cold water for 45 minutes, drained and sliced
2 carrots, peeled and thinly sliced diagonally
225 g/½ lb bean sprouts
225 g/½ lb canned water chestnuts, drained and sliced
125 ml/4 fl oz chicken stock
15 ml/1 tablespoon rice wine or pale dry sherry
15 ml/1 tablespoon soya sauce
350 g/12 oz shrimps, shelled and deveined

1. Cook the vermicelli in boiling water until it is just tender. Drain well, then spread out on paper towels to dry completely.

2. Heat oil in a deep frying pan. Lower the noodles into the oil and deep fry for 3–4 minutes or until golden brown. Drain on paper towels, then arrange in a serving bowl and keep hot.

3. Heat the peanut oil in a frying pan. Add the mushrooms, carrots, bean sprouts and water chestnuts and stir-fry for 5 minutes. Stir in the stock and rice wine and bring to the boil.

4. Add the soya sauce and shrimps and mix well. Cover and simmer for 3–5 minutes or until the mixture is piping hot.

5. Make a well in the centre of the noodles and spoon in the shrimp mixture. Serve immediately.

Serves 3
12

Lo Mein

(Beef and vegetables with noodles)

---

225 g/½ lb rump steak, cut across the grain into thin strips
60 ml/4 tablespoons oyster sauce
125 ml/4 fl oz sesame seed oil
350 g/12 oz egg noodles
4 dried mushrooms, soaked in cold water for 45 minutes, drained and sliced
225 g/½ lb chopped canned bamboo shoots
1 head of Chinese cabbage (pak choy), shredded
225 g/½ lb bean sprouts
5 ml/1 teaspoon brown sugar
30 ml/2 tablespoons soya sauce
125 ml/4 fl oz beef stock
2 spring onions, chopped

1. Put the steak strips into a shallow bowl. Add 45 ml/3 tablespoons of the oyster sauce and 15 ml/1 tablespoon of the oil and toss to coat the steak strips. Marinate for 30 minutes.

2. Meanwhile, cook the noodles in boiling water until just tender. Drain well and keep hot.

3. Heat the remaining oil in a large frying pan. Add the steak strips and stir-fry for 2 minutes. Push the meat to the side of the pan and add the mushrooms, bamboo shoots, cabbage and bean sprouts. Stir-fry for 1 minute.

4. Sprinkle over the sugar, soya sauce, stock and remaining oyster sauce, then add the spring onions and noodles. Mix the meat into the vegetables and stir-fry for a further 2 minutes. Serve hot.

Serves 4

Tan Mein

(Soup noodles)

---

350 g/12 oz egg noodles
20 ml/1½ tablespoons oil
1 small onion, finely sliced
4 cm/1½ in piece of fresh ginger root, peeled and finely chopped
225 g/½ lb lean pork, cut into thin strips
15 ml/1 tablespoon butter
125 g/4 oz button mushrooms
125 g/4 oz shredded cabbage
125 g/4 oz bean sprouts
125 g/4 oz shelled and deveined shrimp
20 ml/1½ tablespoons soya sauce
5 ml/1 teaspoon sugar
300 ml/½ pint water
1 chicken stock cube, crumbled
600 ml/1 pint chicken stock

1. Cook the noodles in boiling water until just tender. Drain and keep hot.

2. Heat the oil in a large frying pan. Add the onion, ginger and pork and stir-fry for 2 minutes. Add the butter. When it has melted, stir in the mushrooms, cabbage, bean sprouts and shrimps. Stir-fry for 1½ minutes. Add the soya sauce and sugar and stir-fry for 1½ minutes. Remove from the heat.

3. Bring the water to the boil in a large saucepan. Stir in the stock cube until dissolved, then add the stock. Return to the boil. Add the noodles and simmer to reheat.

4. Meanwhile, return the frying pan to the heat and stir-fry for 1 minute to reheat. Divide the noodle mixture between serving bowls and spoon over the pork mixture.

Serves 4

Cha Chiang Mein

(Noodles in meat sauce with shredded vegetables)

---

450 g/1 lb egg noodles
45 ml/3 tablespoons oil
1 medium onion, thinly sliced
2 garlic cloves, crushed
4 cm/1½ in piece of fresh ginger root, peeled and finely chopped
350 g/12 oz minced pork or beef
15 ml/1 tablespoon sesame seed oil
75 ml/5 tablespoons soya sauce
30 ml/2 tablespoons rice wine or pale dry sherry
15 ml/1 tablespoon sugar
15 ml/1 tablespoon cornflour
60 ml/4 tablespoons chicken stock
Vegetables
125 g/4 oz shredded cabbage
125 g/4 oz shredded carrots
125 g/4 oz bean sprouts
50 g/2 oz shredded radishes
45 ml/3 tablespoons pickle relish

1. Arrange the shredded vegetables and pickle relish on individual serving plates. Cook the noodles in boiling water until
just tender. Drain and keep hot.

2. Heat the oil in a large frying pan. Add the onion, garlic and
ginger and stir-fry for 1½ minutes. Add the pork or beef and stir-
fry for 3 minutes. Add the sesame seed oil, soya sauce, wine or
sherry and sugar and stir-fry for a further 3 minutes.

3. Dissolve the cornflour in the stock and add to the pan. Cook,
stirring, until the liquid in the pan thickens. Divide the meat
mixture between warmed serving bowls and spoon the noodles
on top. Serve with the shredded vegetables.

Serves 4

Chow Fan

(Fried rice)

---

225 g/½ lb long-grain rice
450 ml/¾ pint water
7.5 ml/1½ teaspoons salt
30 ml/2 tablespoons oil
2 medium onions, chopped
175 g/6 oz cooked ham, finely chopped
30 ml/2 tablespoons cooked peas
2 medium tomatoes, skinned and quartered
225 g/½ lb shelled and deveined shrimp
15 ml/1 tablespoon soya sauce
1 egg, beaten

1. Put the rice into a saucepan with the water and 5 ml/1 teaspoon salt. Bring to the boil, then cover and cook very gently for 15–20 minutes or until the rice is tender and has absorbed all the water. Remove from the heat and keep hot.

2. Heat the oil in a large frying pan. Add the onions and fry until softened. Stir in the ham, peas, tomatoes, shrimps and remaining salt and stir-fry for 1 minute.

3. Add the rice to the pan and stir-fry for 2 minutes. Pour over the soya sauce and egg and stir-fry for a further 2 minutes. Serve hot.

Serves 4

Pork Fried Rice

225 g/½ lb long-grain rice
450 ml/¾ pint water
7.5 ml/1½ teaspoons salt
45 ml/3 tablespoons oil
1 small onion, thinly sliced
4 cm/1½ in piece of fresh ginger root, peeled and finely chopped
2 celery stalks, thinly sliced diagonally
2 small carrots, peeled and thinly sliced
½ head of Chinese cabbage (pak choy), shredded
225 g/½ lb roast pork, cut into thin strips
30 ml/2 tablespoons soya sauce
2 eggs, beaten

1. Put the rice into a saucepan with the water and 1 teaspoon salt. Bring to the boil, then cover and cook very gently for 15–20 minutes or until the rice is tender and has absorbed all the water. Remove from the heat and keep hot.

2. Heat 30 ml/2 tablespoons of the oil in a large frying pan. Add the onion and ginger and stir-fry for 2 minutes. Add the celery and carrots and stir-fry for 3 minutes. Add the cabbage, pork, pepper to taste, soya sauce and rice and mix well. Stir-fry until the mixture is piping hot. Remove from the heat and keep hot.

3. Heat the remaining oil in a small frying pan. Pour in the eggs and sprinkle with the remaining salt. Cook for 2 minutes or until the bottom of the omelette has set, then flip and cook the other side for 2 minutes.

4. Slide the omelette on to a plate and cut into small strips. Serve the rice mixture garnished with the omelette strips.

Serves 4

Egg Foo Yung

4 eggs
15 ml/1 tablespoon soya sauce
30 ml/2 tablespoons butter
1 spring onion, very finely chopped
125 g/4 oz bean sprouts

1. Lightly beat the eggs with the soya sauce and salt and pepper to taste.

2. Melt the butter in a frying pan. Add the spring onion and bean sprouts and stir-fry for 3 minutes.

3. Spread out the vegetables in the pan, then pour over the egg mixture. Cook until set. If liked, the omelette can be placed under a preheated grill to brown the top. Serve hot.

Serves 2

(Top) Pork fried rice
(Bottom) Egg foo yung

MEAT

Beef with Broccoli

450 g/1 lb fillet of beef, cut into thin 7.5 × 5 cm/3 × 2 in pieces
45 ml/3 tablespoons soya sauce
15 ml/1 tablespoon rice wine or pale dry sherry
2.5 cm/1 in piece of fresh ginger root, peeled and finely chopped
60 ml/4 tablespoons oil
125 ml/4 fl oz beef stock
450 g/1 lb broccoli, cut into bite-size pieces
15 ml/1 tablespoon lard
10 ml/2 teaspoons cornflour
30 ml/2 tablespoons water

1. Put the beef pieces in a shallow bowl. Mix together the soya sauce, wine or sherry, ginger and 15 ml/1 tablespoon of the oil. Pour over the meat and turn to coat well. Marinate for 10 minutes.

2. Heat the remaining oil in a large frying pan. Add the meat pieces and stir-fry for 1½ minutes. Remove from the pan.

3. Add the stock to the pan and bring to the boil. Add the broccoli and stir-fry for 1 minute. Cover and cook gently for 4 minutes. Transfer the broccoli to a warmed serving bowl, using a slotted spoon. Keep hot.

4. Add the lard to the pan and melt it. Return the meat pieces to the pan and stir-fry for 30 seconds.

5. Dissolve the cornflour in the water and add to the pan. Stir until the liquid thickens. Pour the beef mixture over the broccoli and serve hot.

Serves 4

Ginger Beef

10 ml/2 teaspoons ground ginger
75 ml/5 tablespoons soya sauce
10 ml/2 teaspoons cornflour
2.5 ml/½ teaspoon sugar
700 g/1½ lb rump steak, thinly sliced across the grain into strips
50 ml/2 fl oz oil
5 cm/2 in piece of fresh ginger root, peeled and chopped
125 g/4 oz diced canned bamboo shoots
4 dried mushrooms, soaked in cold water for 45 minutes, drained and sliced

1. Mix together the ground ginger, soya sauce, cornflour and sugar in a shallow dish. Add the steak strips and turn to coat them well. Marinate for 1 hour.

2. Heat the oil in a large frying pan. Add the ginger root and stir-fry for 3 minutes. Add the steak strips, bamboo shoots and mushrooms and stir-fry for a further 6–8 minutes. Serve hot.

Serves 4

Beef in Fruit Sauce

30 ml/2 tablespoons oil
1 medium onion, thinly sliced
2 garlic cloves, crushed
2.5 cm/1 in piece of fresh ginger root, peeled and chopped
1 × 1.5 kg/3 lb boned leg of beef, cubed
juice of 1 lemon
juice of 2 oranges
60 ml/4 tablespoons soya sauce
300 ml/½ pint red wine
600 ml/1 pint water

1. Preheat the oven to 150°C/300°F (Gas 2). Heat the oil in a flameproof casserole. Add the onion, garlic and ginger and stir-fry for 1 minute. Add the beef cubes, in batches, and brown on all sides.

2. Return all the beef cubes to the casserole, then stir in the remaining ingredients with salt and pepper to taste. Bring to the boil.

3. Cover the casserole and place it in the oven. Cook for 4 hours, stirring once or twice during the cooking period. Serve hot.

Serves 8

Red Cooked Pork

1 × 2 kg/4 lb belly of pork
50 ml/2 fl oz oil
105 ml/7 tablespoons soya sauce
15 ml/1 tablespoon sugar
175 ml/6 fl oz chicken or beef stock
175 ml/6 fl oz red wine

1. Preheat the oven to 170°C/325°F (Gas 3). Cut the pork through the skin into 12 equal pieces. Heat the oil in a flameproof casserole. Add the pork pieces and brown on all sides.

2. Pour off all the oil from the casserole. Add 60 ml/4 tablespoons of the soya sauce and half the sugar, stock and wine. Mix well, turning the pork over to coat with the sauce. Bring to the boil.

3. Transfer the casserole to the oven and cook for 1 hour, turning the meat once.

4. Add the remaining soya sauce, sugar, stock and wine to the casserole and turn the meat over several times. Reduce the oven temperature to 150°C/300°F (Gas 2) and continue cooking for 1 hour, turning the meat once. Serve hot.

Serves 4–6

Pork in Ground Rice

1 × 1 kg/2 lb belly of pork
4 cm/1½ in piece of fresh ginger root, peeled and finely chopped
30 ml/2 tablespoons soya sauce
7.5 ml/1½ teaspoons chilli sauce
150 g/5 oz coarsely ground rice

1. Cut the pork into thin slices, about 7.5 × 4 cm/3 × 1½ inches. Mix together the ginger, soya sauce and chilli sauce and rub over the pork slices to coat both sides. Marinate for 1 hour.

2. Heat a large frying pan. Add the rice and stir-fry until it begins to brown. Remove from the heat. Place the pork slices in the pan and turn to coat with the rice.

3. Arrange the pork slices on a heatproof plate and steam for 35–40 minutes. Alternatively, use an ordinary steamer or Chinese bamboo steamer.

4. Serve the pork hot, with the following dips: tomato-soya sauce (equal quantities of tomato ketchup and soya sauce), garlic-soya (3 finely chopped garlic cloves and 50 ml/2 fl oz soya sauce) and soya-sherry-chilli (45 ml/3 tablespoons each of soya sauce and pale dry sherry and 15 ml/1 tablespoon chilli sauce).

Serves 4

Shao Jou

(Cantonese roast pork)

1.5 kg/3 lb pork fillet, cut into 15 × 4 cm/6 × 1½ in strips
30 ml/2 tablespoons oil
Marinade
1 onion, finely chopped
75 ml/5 tablespoons soya sauce
15 ml/1 tablespoon sugar
15 ml/1 tablespoon rice wine or pale dry sherry
7.5 ml/1½ teaspoons ground ginger
15 ml/1 tablespoon hoisin sauce (optional)

1. Mix together the ingredients for the marinade in a shallow bowl. Add the pork strips and turn to coat well. Marinate for 2 hours.

2. Preheat the oven to 180°C/350°F (Gas 4). Drain the pork, reserving the marinade. Arrange the pork in one layer in a roasting tin. Baste with 15 ml/1 tablespoon of the oil and half the reserved marinade. Roast for 15 minutes.

3. Turn over the pork strips. Baste with the remaining oil and marinade and roast for a further 15 minutes. Cut into very thin slices and serve hot.

Serves 6–8

Double Cooked Pork

1 × 1 kg/2 lb belly of pork
50 ml/2 fl oz oil
1 large green pepper, cored, seeded and cut into thin strips
1 red pepper, cored, seeded and cut into thin strips
3 garlic cloves, crushed
3 spring onions, chopped
1 chilli pepper, seeded and chopped
20 ml/1½ tablespoons soya sauce
10 ml/2 teaspoons sugar
30 ml/2 tablespoons rice wine or pale dry sherry

1. Put the pork in a large saucepan and cover with water. Bring to the boil, then cover the pan and simmer for 1 hour. Drain well. When it is cool enough to handle, cut the pork into thin strips.

2. Heat half the oil in a frying pan. Add the pork strips and stir-fry for 5 minutes. Remove the pork from the pan and pour off all the oil.

3. Heat the remaining oil in the pan. Add the peppers, garlic and spring onions and stir-fry for 2 minutes. Return the pork strips to the pan with the chilli pepper and bean sauce and stir-fry for 1 minute.

4. Add the sugar and wine or sherry and stir-fry for a final 2 minutes. Serve hot.

Serves 4

Ham in Honey Syrup

1 × 1.5 kg/3 lb middle leg of gammon
30 ml/2 tablespoons sugar
105 ml/7 tablespoons water
30 ml/2 tablespoons clear honey
30 ml/2 tablespoons rice wine or pale dry sherry
10 ml/2 teaspoons cherry brandy
10 ml/2 teaspoons cornflour

1. Put the gammon in the upper part of a steamer and steam over boiling water for $2\frac{1}{4}$ hours. Remove the gammon from the steamer. When it is cool enough to handle, cut it into 6 mm/$\frac{1}{4}$ inch slices. Arrange the slices on a heatproof serving plate.

2. Put the sugar, 60 ml/4 tablespoons of the water, the honey, wine or sherry and cherry brandy in a saucepan. Dissolve the cornflour in the remaining water and add to the pan. Bring to the boil, stirring, and simmer until clear and thickened.

3. Pour the honey sauce over the gammon. Steam for a further 3 minutes and serve immediately.

Serves 6–8

Sweet and Sour Pork

15 ml/1 tablespoon soya sauce
50 ml/3½ tablespoons rice wine or pale dry sherry
1 egg white, beaten until frothy
30 ml/2 tablespoons cornflour
450 g/1 lb pork fillet, cut into strips or small cubes
oil for deep frying
Sauce
50 ml/2 fl oz peanut oil
5 cm/2 in piece of fresh ginger root, peeled and chopped
1 red or green pepper, cored, seeded and cut into strips
125 g/4 oz canned pineapple chunks
1 carrot, peeled and sliced
30 ml/2 tablespoons sugar
45 ml/3 tablespoons wine vinegar
30 ml/2 tablespoons soya sauce
30 ml/2 tablespoons tomato purée
10 ml/2 teaspoons lemon or orange juice
15 ml/1 tablespoon cornflour
30 ml/2 tablespoons water

1. Mix together the soya sauce, wine or sherry, egg white and cornflour in a bowl. Add the pork and turn to coat well. Marinate for 1 hour.

2. Heat oil in a deep frying pan. Deep fry the pork, in batches, for 3–4 minutes, or until brown and crisp. Drain.

3. To make the sauce, heat the oil in a frying pan. Add the ginger and pepper and stir-fry for 2 minutes. Add the pork with the pineapple, carrot, sugar, vinegar, soya sauce, tomato purée and lemon or orange juice. Stir-fry for 2 minutes.

4. Dissolve the cornflour in the water and add to the pan. Cook, stirring, until the liquid thickens. Serve hot.

Serves 4

Quick-fried Spinach with Shredded Pork

45 ml/3 tablespoons oil
225 g/¼ lb pork fillet, cut across the grain into thin strips
30 ml/2 tablespoons soya sauce
15 ml/1 tablespoon rice wine or pale dry sherry
5 ml/1 teaspoon sugar
45 ml/3 tablespoons lard
450 g/1 lb spinach, chopped
5 ml/1 teaspoon salt

1. Heat the oil in a large frying pan. Add the pork and stir-fry for 2 minutes. Add the soya sauce, wine or sherry, sugar and pepper to taste and stir-fry for a further 2 minutes. Remove the pork mixture from the pan.

2. Add 30 ml/2 tablespoons of the lard to the pan and melt it. Add the spinach and salt and stir-fry for 3 minutes. Add the remaining lard to the pan and continue stir-frying for 30 seconds. Transfer the spinach to a warmed serving bowl and keep hot.

3. Return the pork to the pan and stir-fry for 1 minute to reheat. Pour the pork over the spinach and serve hot.

Serves 2

Meatball Chop Suey

350 g/12 oz minced pork
50 g/2 oz chopped canned water chestnuts
1 egg
2.5 ml/½ teaspoon sugar
15 ml/1 tablespoon soya sauce
15 ml/1 tablespoon cornflour
oil for deep frying
30 ml/2 tablespoons peanut oil
2 medium onions, thinly sliced
225 g/½ lb cabbage, shredded
300 ml/½ pint chicken stock
225 g/½ lb bean sprouts
½ cucumber, shredded lengthways

1. Mix together the pork, water chestnuts, egg, sugar, soya sauce, cornflour and salt and pepper to taste. Shape the mixture into 10 or 12 small balls.

2. Heat oil in a deep frying pan. Deep fry the meatballs, in batches, for 3–4 minutes or until they are lightly browned and crisp. Drain on paper towels.

3. Heat the peanut oil in a saucepan. Add the onions and cabbage and fry until softened. Stir in the stock and bring to the boil. Simmer for 15 minutes.

4. Spread the bean sprouts over the cabbage mixture and cover with the cucumber. Arrange the meatballs on top. Simmer for a further 8 minutes. Serve hot.

Serves 4

Shredded Pork Stir-fried with Spring Greens

350 g/12 oz pork fillet, cut into thin strips
10 ml/2 teaspoons cornflour
45 ml/3 tablespoons oil
450 g/1 lb spring greens, shredded
15 ml/1 tablespoon lard
50 ml/2 fl oz beef stock
30 ml/2 tablespoons soya sauce
5 ml/1 teaspoon sugar
30 ml/2 tablespoons rice wine or pale dry sherry

1. Rub the pork strips with the cornflour and salt and pepper to taste.

2. Heat the oil in a large frying pan. Add the pork and stir-fry for 3 minutes. Push the pork to the side of the pan and add the greens and lard. Stir-fry for 1 minute.

3. Add the stock, soya sauce and sugar and stir-fry for 3 minutes.

4. Stir the pork strips into the greens. Sprinkle over the wine or sherry and stir-fry for a final 1 minute. Serve hot.

Serves 4

(Left) Meatball chop suey
(Right) Shredded pork stir-fried with spring greens

POULTRY

Lemon Chicken

---

1 × 2 kg/4 lb chicken, skinned
2.5 cm/1 in piece of fresh ginger root, peeled and grated
1 egg, beaten
125 g/4 oz ground rice
oil for deep frying
juice of 1 lemon
1 spring onion, chopped
1 lemon, cut into thin slices
Sauce
125 ml/4 fl oz chicken stock
30 ml/2 tablespoons rice wine or pale dry sherry
7.5 ml/1½ teaspoons sugar

1. Using a cleaver, cut the chicken, through the bones, into 20 or 24 pieces. Rub the ginger and salt to taste into the pieces. Dip them in the beaten egg, then coat with the ground rice.

2. Heat oil in a deep frying pan. Deep fry the chicken pieces, in batches, for 3–5 minutes or until golden brown and crisp. Drain on paper towels.

3. To make the sauce, put all the ingredients in a saucepan and bring to the boil.

4. Arrange the chicken pieces on a warmed serving platter. Pour the sauce over them, then sprinkle over the lemon juice and spring onion. Garnish with the lemon slices and serve hot.

Serves 4–6

Egg-braised Sliced Chicken

4 chicken breasts, skinned, boned and cut into thin strips
10 ml/2 teaspoons sugar
5 ml/1 teaspoon chilli sauce
30 ml/2 tablespoons dry white wine
15 ml/1 tablespoon cornflour
oil for deep frying
3 eggs, beaten
90 ml/6 tablespoons sesame seed oil
15 ml/1 tablespoon chopped parsley
20 ml/1½ tablespoons rice wine or pale dry sherry
20 ml/1½ tablespoons soya sauce
20 ml/1¼ tablespoons lemon juice

1. Rub the chicken strips with salt, pepper, the sugar, chilli sauce, wine and cornflour. Marinate for 1½ hours.

2. Heat oil in a deep frying pan. Deep fry the chicken strips, in batches, for 2 minutes or until golden. Drain on paper towels.

3. Dip the chicken strips into the beaten eggs to coat thickly.

4. Heat the sesame seed oil in a large frying pan. Add the chicken strips, arranging them in one layer if possible, and fry for 2 minutes or until golden brown on all sides.

5. Transfer the chicken to a warmed serving plate and sprinkle with the parsley, wine or sherry, soya sauce and lemon juice. Serve hot.

Serves 4

Szechuan Chicken & Ham

1.75 litres/3 pints chicken stock
4 cm/1¼ in piece of fresh ginger root, peeled and chopped
3 spring onions, chopped
1 × 2 kg/4 lb chicken
4 slices of prosciutto
700 g/1½ lb broccoli spears
15 ml/1 tablespoon soya sauce
5 ml/1 teaspoon cornflour
15 ml/1 tablespoon water

1. Put the stock in a large saucepan with the ginger and spring onions. Bring to the boil. Put the chicken in the pan and add enough boiling water to cover. Return to the boil, then cover and simmer for 40 minutes. Remove the pan from the heat and set aside, still covered. Leave for 2 hours.

2. Drain the chicken, reserving 450 ml/¾ pint of the stock. Cut the chicken into serving pieces and discard the skin. Arrange the chicken on a warmed serving platter. Cut the ham into strips and scatter over the chicken.

3. Pour the reserved stock into the saucepan and bring to the boil. Add the broccoli spears. Return to the boil, then remove from the heat and leave for 5 minutes. Drain the broccoli, reserving 125 ml/4 fl oz of the stock. Arrange the broccoli around the chicken.

4. Pour the reserved stock back into the saucepan and add the soya sauce. Bring to the boil. Dissolve the cornflour in the water and add to the pan. Simmer, stirring, until thickened. Pour this sauce over the chicken and serve.

Serves 4–6

(Top) Egg-braised sliced chicken
(Bottom) Szechuan chicken & ham

Chicken Cubes
Quick-fried with Walnuts

4 chicken breasts, skinned, boned and cut into bite-size pieces
15 ml/1 tablespoon cornflour
5 ml/1 teaspoon salt
1 egg white, beaten until frothy
90 ml/6 tablespoons oil
225 g/½ lb walnut halves
5 ml/1 teaspoon sugar
15 ml/1 tablespoon soya sauce
30 ml/2 tablespoons rice wine or pale dry sherry

1. Rub the chicken pieces with the cornflour and salt. Put into a bowl and pour over the egg white. Toss to coat the chicken pieces evenly.

2. Heat the oil in a frying pan. Add the chicken pieces and stir-fry for 2 minutes. Remove the chicken from the pan.

3. Pour off all but 15 ml/1 tablespoon of oil from the pan. Add the walnuts and stir-fry for 1 minute.

4. Return the chicken to the pan and stir-fry for a further 1 minute. Sprinkle over the sugar, soya sauce and wine or sherry and stir-fry for a final 1½ minutes. Serve hot.

Serves 4

Long-simmered Chicken in White Wine

1 × 2 kg/4 lb chicken
600 ml/1 pint water
300 ml/½ pint dry white wine
1 head of Chinese cabbage (pak choy), shredded
45 ml/3 tablespoons soya sauce
20 ml/1½ tablespoons sesame seed oil
Stuffing
75 g/3 oz long-grain rice
4 spring onions, chopped
4 lean bacon rashers, chopped
5 cm/2 in piece of fresh ginger root, peeled and chopped
1 chicken stock cube, crumbled

1. Preheat the oven to 150°C/300°F (Gas 2). Mix together all the stuffing ingredients with salt and pepper to taste. Stuff into the chicken, then truss. Put the chicken into a flameproof casserole and pour over the water. Bring to the boil.

2. Transfer the casserole to the oven and cook for 1 hour. Add the wine to the casserole and cook for a further 45 minutes or until the chicken is cooked through. Transfer the chicken to a warmed serving platter and keep hot.

3. Add the cabbage to the stock in the casserole and bring to the boil on top of the stove. Simmer for 5 minutes. Serve this as a soup course.

4. When ready to serve the chicken, mix together the soya sauce and sesame seed oil and pour over the chicken.

Serves 4–6

Quick-fried Chicken Cubes in White Sauce

4 chicken breasts, skinned, boned and cut into bite-size pieces
5 ml/1 teaspoon ground ginger
15 ml/1 tablespoon cornflour
15 ml/1 tablespoon butter
30 ml/2 tablespoons oil
125 g/4 oz shelled and deveined shrimps
1 small red pepper, cored, seeded and cut into 12 mm/½ in pieces
1 cucumber, halved lengthways and cut into 12 mm/½ in pieces
Sauce
90 ml/6 tablespoons chicken stock
15 ml/1 tablespoon butter
50 ml/2 fl oz dry white wine
15 ml/1 tablespoon cornflour
50 ml/2 fl oz water
125 ml/4 fl oz single cream

1. Rub the chicken pieces with the ginger, salt, pepper and cornflour.

2. Melt the butter with the oil in a large frying pan. Add the chicken pieces and stir-fry for 30 seconds. Add the shrimps, pepper and cucumber and stir-fry for a further 2 minutes. Remove the pan from the heat.

3. To make the sauce, bring the stock to the boil in a saucepan. Stir in the butter and wine until the butter has melted. Dissolve the cornflour in the water and add to the pan. Simmer, stirring, until thickened. Stir in the cream.

4. Pour the sauce into the pan and stir to mix with the chicken and vegetables. Stir-fry for 2 minutes to reheat. Serve hot.

Serves 4

Stir-fry Duck with Ginger & Pineapple

1 × 2 kg/4 lb duck
5 ml/1 teaspoon ground ginger
75 ml/5 tablespoons soya sauce
50 ml/2 fl oz oil
10 cm/4 in piece of fresh ginger root, peeled and chopped
2 spring onions, chopped
15 ml/1 tablespoon brown sugar
30 ml/2 tablespoons wine vinegar
225 g/½ lb canned pineapple chunks
15 ml/1 tablespoon cornflour
30 ml/2 tablespoons water

1. Preheat the oven to 170°C/325°F (Gas 3). Put the duck on a rack in a roasting tin. Rub all over with pepper, the ground ginger and half the soya sauce. Roast for 2–2½ hours, basting frequently, or until the duck is cooked through and the skin is crisp. Remove from the oven.

2. When the duck is cool enough to handle, cut it into bite-size pieces through the bones, using a cleaver.

3. Heat the oil in a large frying pan. Add the ginger root and stir-fry for 1 minute. Add the duck pieces and spring onions and stir-fry for a further 1 minute.

4. Stir in the sugar, vinegar, pineapple with the can syrup and remaining soya sauce and bring to the boil, stirring well. Simmer for 2 minutes.

5. Dissolve the cornflour in the water and add to the pan. Simmer, stirring, until thickened. Serve hot.

Serves 4

Mongolian Hot Pot

1 × 2 kg/4 lb chicken
1 medium onion, chopped
10 peppercorns
5 ml/1 teaspoon salt
1.2 litres/2 pints water
175 g/6 oz cooked crabmeat
175 g/6 oz prawns, shelled
Vegetables
125 g/4 oz mushrooms, sliced
2 peppers, cored, seeded and sliced
1 small head of Chinese cabbage (pak choy), shredded
Garnishes
275 g/10 oz hot cooked rice
60 ml/4 tablespoons chopped spring onion
10 cm/4 in piece of fresh ginger root, peeled and finely chopped

1. Remove the skin from the chicken and reserve. Take the meat from the carcass and cut it into bite-size pieces. Set aside. Put the chicken carcass, skin and giblets into a saucepan with the onion, peppercorns, salt and water. Bring to the boil, then cover and simmer for 1–1½ hours.

2. Meanwhile, arrange the chicken pieces on a serving platter with the crabmeat, cut into chunks, and prawns. Arrange the vegetables on another serving platter.

3. Put all the garnishes in separate bowls.

4. Strain the stock and pour it into a chafing dish. Arrange the two platters and garnishes around the dish. When the stock is boiling, cook the food in the same way as for a fondue.

Serves 6

FISH & SHELLFISH

Stir-fried Abalone with Chinese Cabbage

---

45 ml/3 tablespoons peanut oil
2.5 cm/1 in piece of fresh ginger root, peeled and chopped
1 small leek, white part only, thinly sliced
1 small head of Chinese cabbage (pak choy), shredded
1.5 ml/¼ teaspoon monosodium glutamate (optional)
10 ml/2 teaspoons soya sauce
20 ml/1½ tablespoons lemon juice
450 g/1 lb canned abalone, drained and sliced

1. Heat the oil in a large frying pan. Add the ginger and leek and stir-fry for 2 minutes. Add the cabbage and stir-fry for 4 minutes.

2. Sprinkle over the monosodium glutamate, if used, salt and pepper to taste, the soya sauce and lemon juice. Stir in the abalone and stir-fry for a further 5 minutes. Serve hot.

Serves 4–6

Carp Steamed with White Wine

1 × 1.5 kg/3 lb carp, cleaned
175 ml/6 fl oz water
175 ml/6 fl oz beef stock
250 ml/8 fl oz dry white wine
45 ml/3 tablespoons soya sauce
20 ml/1½ tablespoons sesame seed oil
1 bunch watercress, shredded (optional)
Stuffing
60 ml/4 tablespoons rice
4 lean bacon rashers, chopped
4 spring onions, finely chopped
1 chicken stock cube, crumbled
7.5 cm/3 in piece of fresh ginger root, peeled and finely chopped

1. Mix together all the stuffing ingredients and stuff into the fish. Sew up with a trussing needle and thread or close with skewers.

2. Place the fish in a heatproof oval dish and pour the water over it. Cover the dish and place over a pan of boiling water. Steam for 45 minutes.

3. Pour the stock and wine over the fish, cover again and steam for a further 45 minutes or until the fish flakes easily.

4. Transfer the fish to a warmed serving platter. Sprinkle over the soya sauce and sesame seed oil and serve hot.

5. To serve the fish cooking liquid as a soup, pour it into a saucepan and add the watercress. Bring to the boil and boil for 2 minutes.

Serves 4–6

Sliced Fish in Tomato Sauce

450 g/1 lb white fish fillets, skinned and cut into 5 × 2.5 cm/2 × 1 in slices
1.5 ml/¼ teaspoon ground ginger
15 ml/1 tablespoon cornflour
1 egg white, beaten until frothy
90 ml/6 tablespoons oil
Sauce
20 ml/1½ tablespoons butter
4 tomatoes, skinned and quartered
40 ml/2½ tablespoons soya sauce
30 ml/2 tablespoons tomato purée
10 ml/2 teaspoons cornflour
90 ml/6 tablespoons chicken or beef stock
30 ml/2 tablespoons rice wine or pale dry sherry
5 ml/1 teaspoon sugar

1. Rub the fish slices with the ginger, cornflour and salt, then coat with the egg white.

2. Heat the oil in a large frying pan. Add the fish slices and fry for 1½ minutes or until golden on both sides. Remove the fish from the pan.

3. Pour off the oil from the pan. Add the butter and melt it. Add the tomato quarters and stir-fry for 2 minutes. Stir in the soya sauce and tomato purée.

4. Dissolve the cornflour in the stock and add to the pan with the wine or sherry and sugar. Simmer, stirring, until thickened.

5. Return the fish slices to the pan and stir-fry for a final 2 minutes. Serve hot.

Serves 3

Velvet Crab

225 g/½ lb vermicelli
oil for deep frying
300 ml/½ pint single cream
250 ml/8 fl oz + 30 ml/2 tablespoons water
5 ml/1 teaspoon sugar
3 eggs, beaten
15 ml/1 tablespoon cornflour
5 ml/1 teaspoon paprika
350 g/12 oz cooked crabmeat, flaked

1. Cook the vermicelli in boiling water until it is just tender. Drain well, then spread out on paper towels to dry completely.

2. Heat oil in a deep frying pan. Lower the noodles into the oil and deep fry for 3–4 minutes or until golden brown. Drain on paper towels, then arrange in a warmed serving bowl and keep hot.

3. Put the cream, 250 ml/8 fl oz water, the sugar and salt and pepper to taste in a saucepan and bring to the boil. Reduce the heat to low and beat in the eggs.

4. Dissolve the cornflour in the remaining water and add to the pan with the paprika. Simmer, stirring, until smooth and thick. Stir in the crabmeat and cook for a further 3 minutes or until the crabmeat is heated through.

5. Spoon the crabmeat mixture over the vermicelli and serve hot.

Serves 4

Cantonese Lobster

1 × 1 kg/2 lb cooked lobster
90 ml/6 tablespoons peanut oil
1 garlic clove, crushed
5 cm/2 in piece of fresh ginger root, peeled and chopped
125 g/4 oz minced pork
250 ml/8 fl oz chicken stock
15 ml/1 tablespoon rice wine or pale dry sherry
15 ml/1 tablespoon soya sauce
5 ml/1 teaspoon sugar
15 ml/1 tablespoon cornflour
30 ml/2 tablespoons water
3 spring onions, chopped
2 eggs, beaten

1. Remove the lobster meat from the shell and cut it into bite-size pieces.

2. Heat half the oil in a large frying pan. Add the garlic and stir-fry for 1 minute. Add the lobster pieces and stir-fry for 3–5 minutes or until they are lightly browned and heated through. Transfer to a warmed serving bowl and keep hot.

3. Heat the remaining oil in the pan. Add the ginger and pork and stir-fry until the pork is lightly browned. Stir in the stock, wine or sherry, soya sauce and sugar and stir-fry for a further 1 minute.

4. Dissolve the cornflour in the water and add to the pan. Stir until the liquid thickens. Stir in the spring onions and stir-fry for 1 minute. Remove the pan from the heat.

5. Pour the eggs over the pork mixture and lift the mixture to allow the eggs to run on to the pan. When the eggs are creamy and lightly 'set', spoon the mixture over the lobster. Serve hot.

Serves 2–4

Quick-fried Prawns with Cashews

15 ml/1 tablespoon rice wine or pale dry sherry
1 egg white, beaten until frothy
20 ml/1½ tablespoons cornflour
2.5 ml/½ teaspoon ground ginger
450 g/1 lb prawns, shelled
50 ml/2 fl oz oil
125 g/4 oz unsalted cashew nuts
5 cm/2 in piece of fresh ginger root, peeled and finely chopped
4 spring onions, finely chopped
75 g/3 oz canned bamboo shoots, finely chopped

1. Put half the wine or sherry, the egg white, 15 ml/1 tablespoon of the cornflour, the ground ginger and salt and pepper to taste in a bowl and beat until smooth. Add the prawns and turn to coat with the batter. Marinate for 30 minutes.

2. Heat the oil in a large frying pan. Add the cashews and stir-fry for 5 minutes or until deep golden.

3. Push the nuts to the side of the pan and add the prawns. Stir-fry for 3 minutes or until crisp. Add the ginger root, spring onions and bamboo shoots and stir-fry for a further 2 minutes.

4. Dissolve the remaining cornflour in the rest of the wine or sherry and add to the pan. Stir until the liquid thickens. Stir the cashews into the prawn mixture and serve hot.

Serves 4

Quick-fried Prawns on Crackling Rice

450 g/1 lb prawns, shelled
15 ml/1 tablespoon cornflour
450 g/1 lb cooked rice
oil for deep frying
Sauce
30 ml/2 tablespoons oil
1 onion, finely chopped
175 ml/6 fl oz beef stock
30 ml/2 tablespoons tomato purée
20 ml/1½ tablespoons soya sauce
20 ml/1½ tablespoons sugar
20 ml/1½ tablespoons wine vinegar
30 ml/2 tablespoons rice wine or pale dry sherry
5 ml/1 teaspoon chilli sauce
20 ml/4 teaspoons cornflour

1. Preheat the oven to 150°C/300°F (Gas 2). Rub the prawns with the cornflour and salt and pepper. Spread the rice in a dish and put into the oven to dry out for 15 minutes.

2. Meanwhile, heat the oil in a saucepan. Add the onion and fry until softened. Stir in the stock, purée, soya sauce, sugar, vinegar, wine and chilli sauce. Dissolve the cornflour in water and add to the pan. Bring to the boil, and simmer until smooth.

3. Heat oil in a deep frying pan. Deep fry the prawns for 1 minute. Drain, then add to the sauce. Cook, stirring, for 2 minutes.

4. Re-heat the oil and lower in the rice and deep fry for 1½ minutes. Drain and arrange on a platter. Pour over the sauce.

Serves 4

Prawn Balls with Green Peas

450 g/1 lb prawns, shelled, and finely chopped
5 ml/1 teaspoon ground ginger
30 ml/2 tablespoons fresh breadcrumbs
125 g/4 oz + 5 ml/1 teaspoon cornflour
1 egg yolk
oil for deep frying
Sauce
30 ml/2 tablespoons peanut oil
4 cm/1½ in piece of fresh ginger root, peeled and finely chopped
15 ml/1 tablespoon wine vinegar
15 ml/1 tablespoon soya sauce
15 ml/1 tablespoon tomato purée
10 ml/2 teaspoons brown sugar
125 ml/4 fl oz chicken stock
125 g/4 oz frozen peas, thawed
15 ml/1 tablespoon cornflour

1. Mix together the prawns, ginger, breadcrumbs, the 5 ml/1 teaspoon cornflour and the egg yolk. Shape the mixture into walnut-sized balls and coat with the remaining cornflour.

2. Heat oil in a deep frying pan. Deep fry the prawn balls, in batches, until they are golden brown and crisp. Drain.

3. To make the sauce, heat the oil in a large frying pan. Add the ginger and stir-fry for 1 minute. Stir in the vinegar, soya sauce, purée, sugar and stock and bring to the boil. Stir in the peas, then add the balls to the sauce. Cook, stirring, for 2 minutes.

4. Dissolve the cornflour in water and add to the pan. Cook, stirring, until the sauce thickens. Serve hot.

Serves 4

Prawn Fritters

90 ml/6 tablespoons cornflour
5 ml/1 teaspoon salt
1.5 ml/¼ teaspoon cayenne pepper
2 eggs, separated
45 ml/3 tablespoons water
oil for deep frying
450 g/1 lb Dublin Bay prawns, shelled but tails left on and deveined
2 lemons, cut into wedges
Sauce
15 ml/1 tablespoon wine vinegar
15 ml/1 tablespoon brown sugar
15 ml/1 tablespoon tomato purée
15 ml/1 tablespoon soya sauce
15 ml/1 tablespoon oil
50 ml/2 fl oz rice wine or pale dry sherry
1.5 ml/¼ teaspoon salt
15 ml/1 tablespoon cornflour
125 ml/4 fl oz water

1. Mix together the cornflour, salt, cayenne, egg yolks and water to make a smooth batter. Set aside for 20 minutes.

2. Meanwhile, make the sauce. Put the vinegar, sugar, tomato purée, soya sauce, oil, wine or sherry and salt in a saucepan and bring to the boil, stirring. Dissolve the cornflour in the water and add to the pan. Simmer, stirring, until the sauce thickens. Beat the egg whites until stiff and fold into the batter.

3. Heat oil in a deep frying pan. Holding the prawns by their tails, dip them into the batter, then drop them into the oil. Fry for 3 minutes or until golden brown. Drain on paper towels.

4. Reheat the sauce if necessary, then serve with the hot fritters, accompanied by the lemon wedges.

Serves 6

VEGETABLES

Stir-fry Mixed Vegetables

50 ml/2 fl oz sesame seed oil
4 cm/1½ in piece of fresh ginger root, peeled and chopped
1 large leek, cut into 2.5 cm/1 in pieces
2 large carrots, peeled and thinly sliced
1 large red pepper, cored, seeded and cut into thin strips
1 cucumber, halved lengthways, seeded and cut into 2.5 cm/1 in pieces
4 button mushrooms, sliced

1. Heat the oil in a large frying pan. Add the ginger and stir-fry for 2 minutes.

2. Add the leek and carrots and stir-fry for 2 minutes.

3. Add the pepper, cucumber and mushrooms and continue stir-frying for 3 minutes or until the vegetables are hot but still crisp. Serve hot.

Serves 4

Szechuan Bean Curd with Spicy Meat & Vegetables

50 ml/2 fl oz peanut oil
1 garlic clove, crushed
7.5 cm/3 in piece of fresh ginger root, peeled and finely chopped
4 spring onions, finely chopped
4 dried mushrooms, soaked in cold water for 45 minutes, drained and chopped
5 ml/1 teaspoon red pepper flakes
2 dried red chilli peppers, seeded and chopped
175 g/6 oz minced beef
30 ml/2 tablespoons soya sauce
250 ml/8 floz + 30 ml/2 tablespoons chicken stock
3 cakes fresh bean curd, mashed
15 ml/1 tablespoon cornflour

1. Heat the oil in a large frying pan. Add the garlic, ginger, spring onions and mushrooms and stir-fry for 3 minutes. Add the red pepper flakes and chilli peppers and stir-fry for 1 minute.

2. Add the beef and fry until it is lightly browned. Stir in the soya sauce and 250 ml/8 fl oz of stock and bring to the boil.

3. Add the bean curd and stir-fry for 5 minutes.

4. Dissolve the cornflour in the remaining stock and add to the pan. Stir until the mixture thickens. Serve hot.

Serves 6

Stir-braised Cauliflower with Parsley

50 ml/2 fl oz peanut oil
1 medium head of cauliflower, broken into florets
1 medium onion, chopped
1 garlic clove, crushed
2.5 ml/½ teaspoon ground ginger
1.5 ml/¼ teaspoon 5-spice powder
175 ml/6 fl oz vegetable or beef stock
30 ml/2 tablespoons rice wine or pale dry sherry
60 ml/4 tablespoons chopped parsley

1. Heat the oil in a large frying pan. Add the cauliflower, onion, garlic and ginger and stir-fry for 5 minutes.

2. Stir in the 5-spice powder, stock, wine or sherry and parsley and bring to the boil. Cover and simmer for 7 minutes, stirring occasionally. Serve hot.

Serves 6

ITALIAN COOKING

CONTENTS

Minestrone

75 g/3oz dried red kidney beans, soaked overnight
50 g/2 oz dried chick peas, soaked overnight
175 g/6 oz salt pork, diced
50 ml/2 fl oz olive oil
2 medium onions, chopped
1 garlic clove, crushed
2 medium potatoes, peeled and diced
4 carrots, cut into 12 mm/½ in slices
4 celery stalks, cut into 12 mm/½ in slices
½ small head of green cabbage, cored and shredded
6 tomatoes, skinned, seeded and chopped
6 pints chicken stock
75 g/3 oz macaroni

1. Drain the beans and chick peas and put them in a saucepan with fresh cold water. Bring to the boil and simmer for 45 minutes or until they are almost tender. Drain well.

2. Fry the salt pork in a large saucepan until it is crisp and has rendered most of its fat. Remove the dice from the pan.

3. Add the oil to the fat in the pan and heat it. Add the onions and garlic and fry until softened. Stir in the potatoes, carrots and celery and fry for a further 5 minutes, stirring. Add the cabbage and tomatoes and cook for 5 minutes longer.

4. Add the stock, seasoning to taste, beans and chick peas and bring to the boil. Cover and simmer for 35 minutes. Add macaroni and continue simmering, uncovered, for 10–15 minutes, until the macaroni is *al dente*.

Serves 8

Zuppa alla Pavese

(Bread and egg soup)

---

50 g/2 oz butter
4 slices of French or Italian bread
45 ml/3 tablespoons grated Parmesan cheese
4 eggs
900 ml/1½ pints canned beef consommé

1. Melt the butter in a frying pan. Add the bread slices and fry until they are golden brown on both sides.

2. Place the bread slices in four heated soup bowls and sprinkle with the cheese.

3. Break an egg into each bowl so that it falls to the side of, not on top of, the bread.

4. Bring the consommé to the boil, then ladle it gently over the egg and bread. Serve immediately.

Serves 4

Variation

Zuppa di fontina (Bread and cheese soup): Use 75 g/3 oz of butter to fry 12 slices of French or Italian bread until golden brown. Use the slices to line the bottom and sides of an ovenproof soup tureen or casserole. Place a slice of Fontina cheese on each slice of bread. Pour over 1.5 litres/2½ pints of boiling beef consommé or stock. Put the tureen or casserole in a 180°C/350°F (Gas 4) oven and cook for 10 minutes. Serves 6–8.

Zuppa di Fagioli Fiorentina

(Bean and macaroni soup)

---

225 g/½ lb dried white haricot beans, soaked overnight
125 g/4 oz macaroni pieces
450 g/1 lb lean bacon, chopped
1 large onion, grated
2 garlic cloves, crushed
400 g/14 oz canned tomatoes
1.75 litres/3 pints light stock
30 ml/2 tablespoons chopped parsley
grated Parmesan cheese to serve

1. Put all the ingredients, except the parsley and cheese, into a saucepan and bring to the boil, stirring frequently. Cover and simmer for 1½–2 hours or until the beans are tender.

2. Add seasoning to taste, then ladle into a warmed tureen. Garnish with the parsley and serve hot, with grated Parmesan cheese.

Serves 6

Insalata di Pomodore e Mozzarella

(Tomato and mozzarella salad)

---

450 g/1 lb tomatoes, thinly sliced
225 g/½ lb mozzarella cheese, thinly sliced
75 ml/5 tablespoons olive oil
5 ml/1 teaspoon dried basil

1. Arrange the tomato slices around the edge of a serving plate. Pile the cheese slices in the centre.

2. Mix together the oil, basil and seasoning to taste and pour over the tomatoes. Leave for 5 minutes, then serve.

Serves 4

Variation

Insalata di pomodoro e salami (Tomato and salami salad): Omit the mozzarella cheese and use about 175 g/6 oz salami, thinly sliced. Arrange the tomato and salami slices in rows on a serving plate and separate the rows with chopped stoned black olives. For the dressing, mix together 90 ml/6 tablespoons olive oil, 45 ml/3 tablespoons white wine vinegar, 5 ml/1 teaspoon lemon juice, 1 crushed garlic clove and seasoning. Pour this dressing over the tomato and salami slices, then chill for 15 minutes. Sprinkle with 5 ml/1 teaspoon dried basil just before serving. Serves 6.

Bagna Cauda

(Anchovy and garlic dip)

---

125 g/4 oz butter
30 ml/2 tablespoons olive oil
3 garlic cloves, finely chopped
6 anchovy fillets, finely chopped
150 ml/¼ pint cream
vegetables for dipping (see below)

1. Melt the butter with the oil in a saucepan. Add the garlic and anchovies and cook gently, stirring and mashing with a wooden spoon until the ingredients have almost formed a paste.

2. Stir in the cream and heat through without boiling.

3. Pour the dip into a chafing dish and serve with vegetables for dipping: sticks of carrot, celery and cucumber, cauliflower florets, radishes and green and red pepper rings.

Serves 4–6

Caponata

(Tangy aubergine appetizer)

---

4 small aubergines, peeled and diced
salt
125 ml/4 fl oz olive oil
4 celery stalks, thinly sliced
2 large onions, thinly sliced
125 g/4 oz tomato purée
50 ml/2 fl oz water
15 ml/1 tablespoon capers
50 g/2 oz stoned green olives, chopped
90 ml/6 tablespoons red wine vinegar
15 ml/1 tablespoon sugar

1. Put the aubergines in a colander and sprinkle them with salt. Leave to drain for 30 minutes, then rinse and pat dry with paper towels.

2. Heat all but 30 ml/ 2 tablespoons of the oil in a frying pan. Add the aubergine dice and fry until softened and brown. Remove the dice from the pan with a slotted spoon and drain on paper towels.

3. Heat the remaining oil in the pan. Add the celery and onions and fry until lightly browned. Stir in the tomato purée and water. Bring to the boil, then cover and simmer for 15 minutes.

4. Add the capers, olives, vinegar and sugar to the pan and mix well. Stir in the aubergine dice. Continue to simmer gently for 20 minutes, stirring occasionally.

5. Remove from the heat and cool, then chill and serve cold.

Serves 4–6

Fagioli con Tonno

(Bean and tuna salad)

---

450 g/1 lb dried white haricot beans, soaked overnight
30 ml/2 tablespoons olive oil
7.5 ml/1½ teaspoons white wine vinegar
5 ml/1 teaspoon lemon juice
1 medium onion, finely chopped
1 garlic clove, crushed
7.5 ml/1½ teaspoons dried basil
200 g/7 oz canned tuna fish, drained and flaked
6 black olives, stoned

1. Drain the beans and put them in a saucepan. Cover with fresh cold water and bring to the boil. Simmer for 1–1½ hours or until they are just tender. Drain well and cool.

2. Mix together the oil, vinegar, lemon juice, onion, garlic, basil and seasoning to taste in a salad bowl. Add the beans and stir well to coat with the dressing.

3. Fold in the tuna fish and garnish with the olives.

Serves 4–6

PASTA, PIZZE & RICE

Fettuccine Alfredo

(Noodles with cheese and cream)

---

450 g/1 lb fettuccine
50 g/2 oz butter
50 g/2 oz Parmesan cheese, grated
250 ml/8 fl oz whipping cream, warmed

1. Cook the fettuccine in boiling water until it is *al dente*. Drain well and tip into a warmed serving bowl.

2. Add the butter, cheese, cream and seasoning to taste and toss well until the butter has melted and all the ingredients are combined. Serve hot.

Serves 4

Tagliatelle Verde con Salsa di Funghi

(Green noodles with mushroom sauce)

450 g/1 lb tagliatelle verde
40 g/1½ oz butter
1 small onion, finely chopped
1 garlic clove, crushed
15 ml/1 tablespoon chopped parsley
275 g/10 oz mushrooms, thinly sliced
20 ml/1½ tablespoons flour
90 ml/6 tablespoons chicken stock

1. Cook the tagliatelle in boiling water until it is *al dente*.

2. Meanwhile, melt 30 ml/2 tablespoons of the butter in a saucepan. Add the onion, garlic and parsley and fry until the onion is softened. Add the mushrooms and fry for a further 2 minutes.

3. Stir in the flour, then the stock. Simmer, stirring well, for about 5 minutes. If the sauce is too thick, add a little more stock. Season to taste.

4. Drain the tagliatelle well and pile it on a warmed serving plate. Stir the remaining butter into the sauce and pour it over the tagliatelle. Serve hot.

Serves 4

Spaghetti Bolognese

(*Spaghetti with meat sauce*)

4 bacon rashers, chopped
1 medium onion, finely chopped
1 carrot, finely chopped
½ celery stalk, finely chopped
225 g/½ lb minced beef
125 g/¼ lb chicken livers, finely chopped
15 ml/1 tablespoon tomato purée
150 ml/¼ pint white wine
250 ml/8 fl oz beef stock
pinch of grated nutmeg
450 g/1 lb spaghetti
15 ml/1 tablespoon butter
grated Parmesan cheese to serve

1. Fry the bacon in a saucepan until it has rendered its fat. Add the vegetables and fry until they are lightly browned. Add the beef and fry until it is browned and crumbly. Stir in the chicken livers and continue frying for 3 minutes.

2. Pour off any excess fat from the pan, then stir in the tomato purée, wine, stock, nutmeg and seasoning to taste. Bring to the boil. Cover and simmer gently for 30–40 minutes or until the sauce is thick and rich. Taste and adjust the seasoning.

3. About 10 minutes before the sauce is ready, cook the spaghetti in boiling water until it is *al dente*. Drain well, then tip it into a warmed serving bowl. Add the butter and toss to coat the strands of spaghetti.

4. Pour the sauce over the spaghetti and serve hot, with grated Parmesan cheese.

Serves 4

Spaghetti Vongole

(Spaghetti with clam sauce)

---

45 ml/3 tablespoons olive oil
2 garlic cloves, crushed
15 ml/1 tablespoon finely chopped capers
1 small onion, chopped
450 g/1 lb canned tomatoes, drained
2.5 ml/½ teaspoon dried basil
450 g/1 lb spaghetti
425 g/15 oz canned minced clams, drained
15 ml/1 tablespoon chopped parsley
lemon wedges to serve

1. Heat the oil in a saucepan and fry the garlic, capers and onion until the onion is softened. Stir in the tomatoes, basil and seasoning to taste, cover and simmer gently for 30 minutes.

2. About 10 minutes before the sauce is ready, cook the spaghetti in boiling water until it is *al dente*.

3. Add the clams and parsley to the tomato sauce and heat through gently, stirring well.

4. Drain the spaghetti and tip it into a warmed serving bowl. Pour over the clam sauce and garnish with lemon wedges.

Serves 4–6

Cannelloni

(Cannelloni with beef and spinach)

---

2 × 400g/14 oz cans tomato sauce
12 oven-ready cannelloni tubes
25 g/1 oz Parmesan cheese, grated
Filling
30 ml/2 tablespoons olive oil
1 small onion, finely chopped
2 garlic cloves, crushed
225 g/½ lb minced beef
275 g/10 oz frozen chopped spinach, cooked and drained
1 egg
White sauce
30 ml/2 tablespoons butter
30 ml/2 tablespoons flour
250 ml/8 fl oz milk

1. To make the filling, heat the oil in a frying pan. Add the onion and garlic and fry until softened. Add the beef and fry until it is browned. Remove from the heat. Pour off the excess fat from the pan, then mix in the remaining filling ingredients.

2. Preheat the oven to 190°C/375°F (Gas 5). Heat the tomato sauce until hot. Stuff the cannelloni tubes with the filling.

3. Now make the white sauce. Melt the butter in a saucepan. Remove from the heat and stir in the flour. Return to the heat and cook for 1 minute, then gradually stir in the milk. Bring to a boil, stirring, and simmer until thickened.

4. Pour about one-third of the tomato sauce over the bottom of a baking dish. Arrange the cannelloni in the dish and cover with the white sauce. Pour over the remaining sauce and sprinkle the cheese on top. Bake for 30 minutes and serve hot.

Serves 4

Lasagne

4 bacon rashers, chopped
1 medium onion, finely chopped
1 carrot, finely chopped
225 g/½ lb minced beef
125 g/¼ lb chicken livers, finely chopped
150 ml/¼ pint white wine
250 ml/8 fl oz beef stock
225 g/½ lb oven ready lasagne sheets
225 g/½ lb mozzarella cheese, thinly sliced
75 g/3 oz Parmesan cheese, grated
White sauce
30 ml/2 tablespoons butter
30 ml/2 tablespoons flour
250 ml/8 fl oz milk

1. Fry the bacon in a saucepan until it has rendered its fat. Add the vegetables and beef and fry until browned. Stir in the chicken livers and continue frying for 3 minutes.

2. Stir in the wine, stock and seasoning to taste. Bring to the boil. Cover and simmer for 30–40 minutes or until thick.

3. Preheat the oven to 200°C/400°F (Gas 6). Make the white sauce. Melt the butter in a saucepan. Remove from the heat and stir in the flour. Return to the heat and cook for 1 minute, then gradually stir in the milk. Bring to the boil, stirring, and simmer until thickened.

4. Line a greased baking dish with about one-quarter of the lasagne sheets. Spread over half the meat and cover with half the mozzarella. Top with lasagne sheets, then half the white sauce and sprinkle with one-third of the Parmesan. Repeat until the ingredients are used up. Bake for about 30 minutes or until the dish is piping hot.

Serves 4

Risotto Milanese

(Saffron rice)

---

50 g/2 oz butter
30 ml/2 tablespoons chopped beef marrow
1 onion, sliced
450 g/1 lb long-grain or Italian rice
90 ml/6 tablespoons dry white wine
1.2 litres/2 pints boiling beef stock
2.5 ml/½ teaspoon crushed saffron threads soaked in 15 ml/1 tablespoon hot water
50 g/2 oz Parmesan cheese, grated

1. Melt 45 ml/3 tablespoons of the butter in a saucepan and fry the marrow and onion until the onion is softened. Add the rice and cook gently, stirring, for 5 minutes.

2. Stir in the wine and about one-third of the stock. Regulate the heat so that the rice is bubbling all the time. Stir occasionally. When the rice swells and the liquid has been absorbed, add another one-third of the stock.

3. Continue cooking, stirring occasionally, until the rice has absorbed all the liquid. Add the remaining stock and cook until the rice is tender and moist.

4. Stir in the saffron, cheese, remaining butter and seasoning to taste and heat through gently, stirring. Serve hot.

Serves 4–6

Risi e Bisi

(Rice with peas)

---

4 bacon rashers
50 g/2 oz butter
1 onion, thinly sliced
450 g/1 lb long-grain or Italian rice
350 g/12 oz shelled fresh peas
90 ml/6 tablespoons dry white wine
1.2 litres/2 pints boiling chicken stock
125 g/4 oz Parmesan cheese, grated

1. Fry the bacon in a saucepan until it has rendered its fat and is crisp. Remove the bacon from the pan and crumble it.

2. Add half the butter to the pan and melt it. Add the onion and fry until softened. Add the rice and peas and cook gently, stirring, for 5 minutes.

3. Stir in the wine and about one-third of the stock. Regulate the heat so that the rice is bubbling all the time. Stir occasionally. When the rice swells and the liquid has been absorbed, add another one-third of the stock.

4. Continue cooking, stirring occasionally, until the rice has absorbed all the liquid. Add the remaining stock and cook until the rice is tender and moist.

5. Stir in the bacon, cheese, remaining butter and seasoning to taste and heat through gently, stirring. Serve hot.

Serves 4–6

Pizza con Pepperoni

(Pepperoni pizzas)

---

175 g/6 oz mozzarella cheese, sliced
1 pepperoni sausage, thinly sliced
Dough
25 g/1 oz dry yeast
1.5 ml/¼ teaspoon sugar
125 ml/4 fl oz + 30 ml/2 tablespoons lukewarm water
225 g/8 oz plain flour
5 ml/1 teaspoon salt
Tomato sauce
30 ml/2 tablespoons olive oil
1 small onion, finely chopped
450 g/1 lb canned tomatoes
125 g/4 oz tomato purée
2.5 ml/½ teaspoon dried basil

1. First make the dough. Mix together the yeast, sugar and 30 ml/2 tablespoons of water. Sift the flour and salt into a bowl. Add the frothing yeast and the remaining water and mix to make a smooth dough. Knead for 10 minutes or until elastic. Leave to rise for 1 hour or until almost doubled in bulk.

2. Meanwhile, make the tomato sauce. Heat the oil in a saucepan and fry the onion until softened. Stir in the remaining sauce ingredients, cover and simmer for 30 minutes.

3. Preheat the oven to 230°C/450°F (Gas 8). Punch down the dough and knead for 3 minutes. Divide it in half and roll out to ¼ in thick. Place on greased baking sheets.

4. Spread the tomato sauce over the dough rounds, then cover with the cheese slices. Arrange the pepperoni slices on top. Bake for 15–20 minutes or until the crust is crisp.

Serves 2

Pizza Margherita

(Tomato and cheese pizzas)

---

6 tomatoes, thinly sliced
175 g/6 oz mozzarella cheese, sliced
15 ml/1 tablespoon dried basil
10 ml/2 teaspoons olive oil
Dough
25 g/1 oz dry yeast
1.5 ml/¼ teaspoon sugar
125 ml/4 fl oz + 30 ml/2 tablespoons lukewarm water
225 g/8 oz plain flour
5 ml/1 teaspoon salt

1. First make the dough. Using a fork, mix together the yeast, sugar and 30 ml/2 tablespoons of the water. Sift the flour and salt into a bowl. Add the frothing yeast and the remaining water and mix to make a smooth dough. Knead for 10 minutes until elastic. Leave to rise for 1 hour or until almost doubled in bulk.

2. Preheat the oven to 230°C/450°F (Gas 8). Punch down the dough and knead for 3 minutes. Divide it in half and roll out to 6/mm/¼ in thick. Place on greased baking sheets.

3. Arrange the tomato slices in decorative lines on each dough round and separate them with overlapping cheese slices. Sprinkle over the basil and seasoning to taste, then dribble over the olive oil. Bake for 15–20 minutes or until the crust is crisp.

Serves 2

MEAT & POULTRY

Bistecca a la Fiorentina

(Grilled steaks, Florence-style)

---

4 sirloin or T-Bone steaks, at least 2.5 cm/1 in thick
50 g/2 oz butter, cut into dice
60 ml/4 tablespoons olive oil

1. Preheat the grill to its highest setting. Arrange the steaks in the grill pan and scatter over half the butter dice.

2. Grill for 3 minutes, turn over the steaks and scatter over the remaining dice. Grill for 3 minutes.

3. Reduce the grill to moderate and cook for a further 3 minutes on each side. This will produce rare steaks: double the cooking time for well done.

4. About 1 minute before the end of the cooking time, rub salt and freshly ground black pepper to taste over the steaks and brush them with the olive oil.

5. Serve hot, with mixed salad and jacket potato.

Serves 4

Manzo Stufato

(Beef stew with red wine)

---

1 kg/2 lb braising steak, cut into cubes
1 large onion, sliced
4 bacon rashers, chopped
250 ml/8 fl oz beef stock
Marinade
1 onion, sliced
3 garlic cloves, sliced
6 peppercorns, lightly crushed
1 bay leaf
1 thyme sprig
250 ml/8 fl oz red wine
1.5 ml/¼ teaspoon salt

1. Mix together the ingredients for the marinade in a plastic bag. Add the beef cubes. Seal the bag, then marinate in the refrigerator for 5–6 hours or overnight, turning the bag over occasionally.

2. Drain the beef cubes, reserving the marinade. Pat the beef cubes dry with paper towels. Strain the marinade.

3. Fry the onion with the bacon in a saucepan until the onion is softened and the bacon has rendered its fat. Add the beef cubes, in batches, and brown on all sides.

4. Stir in the reserved strained marinade and the stock and bring to the boil. Cover tightly and simmer gently for 2 hours or until the meat is tender and the sauce is thick and reduced. Taste and adjust the seasoning before serving.

Serves 4–6

Abbacchio Brodettato

(Lamb with egg sauce)

---

50 g/2 oz butter
1 kg/2 lb boned lamb (preferably from the leg), cubed
1 small onion, finely chopped
2 garlic cloves, crushed
175 ml/6 fl oz dry white wine
125 ml/4 fl oz chicken stock
5 ml/1 teaspoon dried sage
2 egg yolks
1.5 ml/¼ teaspoon grated lemon rind
juice of 2 lemons
parsley sprigs to garnish

1. Melt the butter in a saucepan. Add the lamb cubes, in batches, and brown on all sides. Remove the lamb cubes from the pan with a slotted spoon.

2. Add the onion and garlic to the pan and fry until the onion is softened. Stir in the wine, stock, sage and seasoning to taste and bring to the boil.

3. Return the lamb cubes to the pan and stir into the sauce. Cover and simmer for 1½ hours or until the lamb is tender.

4. Lightly beat the egg yolks with the lemon rind and juice and seasoning. Stir about 45 ml/3 tablespoons of the sauce into the egg yolk mixture, then stir this into the sauce in the pan. Cook gently, without boiling, until the sauce has thickened. Serve garnished with parsley sprigs.

Serves 4–6

Costoletta di Maiale alla Milanese

(Breaded pork chops)

---

4 pork chops, trimmed of excess fat
45 ml/3 tablespoons lemon juice
40 g/1½ oz flour
2 eggs
50 g/2 oz fine dry breadcrumbs
25 g/1 oz Parmesan cheese, grated
50 g/2 oz butter
lemon quarters to garnish

1. Lay the pork chops on a plate in one layer and sprinkle them with the lemon juice. Leave for 10 minutes.

2. Pat the chops dry with paper towels. Mix the flour with seasoning to taste and use to coat the chops.

3. Lightly beat the eggs in a shallow dish. Mix together the breadcrumbs and cheese on a sheet of greaseproof paper. Dip the chops first in the egg, then coat them all over with the crumb mixture. Chill for 15 minutes.

4. Melt the butter in a large frying pan. Add the chops and fry for about 15–20 minutes on each side or until golden brown and cooked through. Serve garnished with lemon quarters.

Serves 4

Costoletta alla Pizzaiola

(Pork chops in tomato and pepper sauce)

---

6 pork chops, about 2.5 cm/1 in thick
50 ml/2 fl oz oil
2 garlic cloves, crushed
7.5 ml/1½ teaspoons dried basil
150 ml/¼ pint red wine
450 g/1 lb canned tomatoes, chopped with their juice
45 ml/3 tablespoons tomato purée
45 ml/3 tablespoons butter
3 green peppers, seeded and chopped
1 onion, sliced
225 g/½ lb button mushrooms
20 ml/1½ tablespoons cornflour dissolved in 30 ml/2 tablespoons water

1. Rub the chops with salt and pepper. Heat the oil in a large frying pan and fry the chops until they are browned on both sides. Remove from the pan.

2. Pour off all but a thin film of oil from the pan. Add the garlic and herb and stir to mix with the oil. Stir in the wine and bring to the boil. Stir in the tomatoes and tomato purée. Return the chops to the pan and coat with the tomato mixture. Cover and simmer for 40 minutes, basting occasionally.

3. Melt the butter in another frying pan. Add the peppers and onion and fry until softened. Stir in the mushrooms and continue frying for 3 minutes. Stir the vegetables into the pan mixture. Continue cooking, covered, for 15 minutes or until the chops are tender.

4. Transfer the chops to a warmed serving platter. Stir the dissolved cornflour into the sauce and simmer, stirring, until thickened. Pour the sauce over the chops.

Serves 6

96

Polpette

(Veal meatballs)

---

50 g/2 oz fresh breadcrumbs
milk
450 g/1 lb stewing veal, cubed
2 garlic cloves
4 parsley sprigs
2 thin strips of lemon rind
2 eggs, beaten
25 g/1 oz Parmesan cheese, grated
1.5 ml/¼ teaspoon grated nutmeg
50 g/2 oz flour
90 ml/6 tablespoons oil

1. Sprinkle the breadcrumbs with a little milk to moisten them, then leave to soak for 10 minutes. Press all the excess milk out of the breadcrumbs.

2. Put the breadcrumbs, veal, garlic, parsley and lemon rind through the meat mincer, or use a food processor. Beat the eggs, cheese, nutmeg and seasoning to taste into the veal mixture.

3. Flour your hands, then shape the veal mixture into balls the size of walnuts. Coat the balls with the flour.

4. Heat the oil in a frying pan and fry the meatballs, in batches, for about 6–10 minutes or until they are crisp and golden all over and cooked through. Drain on paper towels.

5. Serve hot, on a bed of lettuce leaves.

Serves 2

Osso Buco

(Stewed veal shank)

---

75 g/3 oz flour
1.5 kg/3 lb veal knuckle, sawn into 7.5 cm/3 in pieces
125 g/4 oz butter
1 large onion, sliced
450 g/1 lb canned tomatoes
30 ml/2 tablespoons tomato purée
175 ml/6 fl oz dry white wine
5 ml/1 teaspoon sugar
Gremolada
15 ml/1 tablespoon finely grated lemon rind
2 garlic cloves, crushed
30 ml/2 tablespoons chopped parsley

1. Mix the flour with seasoning to taste and use to coat the veal pieces. Melt the butter in a saucepan and fry the veal pieces, in batches, until they are browned on all sides. Remove the veal from the pan.

2. Add the onion to the pan and fry until softened. Stir in the undrained tomatoes, the tomato purée, wine, sugar and seasoning to taste and bring to the boil.

3. Return the veal pieces to the pan. Cover and simmer gently for $1\frac{1}{2}$–2 hours or until the veal is so tender that the meat is almost falling off the bones.

4. Mix together the ingredients for the gremolada and stir into the veal mixture. Cook for a further 1 minute, then serve.

Serves 6

99

Vitello Tonnato

(Cold veal with tuna sauce)

---

1 × 1.5 kg/3 lb boned loin of veal
3 garlic cloves, halved
3 anchovy fillets, halved
1 medium onion, sliced
2 carrots, sliced
200 g/7 oz canned tuna fish
300 ml/½ pint veal or chicken stock
175 ml/6 fl oz dry white wine
45 ml/3 tablespoons white wine vinegar
Sauce
125 ml/4 fl oz mayonnaise
2 hard-boiled egg yolks, strained
45 ml/3 tablespoons whipped cream

1. Preheat the oven to 180°C/350°F (Gas 4). Make six incisions in the meat and insert half a garlic clove and half an anchovy fillet in each. Put the meat in a flameproof casserole and add the remaining non-sauce ingredients.

2. Bring to the boil, then cover the casserole tightly and transfer it to the oven. Cook for 1½–1¾ hours or until the veal is tender. Remove from the oven and leave the veal to cool in the liquid.

3. Transfer the veal to a carving board and carve it into thin slices. Arrange these on a large serving platter.

4. Strain the cooking liquid into a bowl, rubbing the vegetables and tuna through the strainer. Discard all but 250 ml/8 fl oz of the liquid, and beat in the mayonnaise, egg yolks and cream.

5. Pour the sauce over the veal slices to cover them. Chill for 8 hours or overnight. Serve garnished with capers and olives.

Serves 6–8

Scaloppine alla Marsala

(Veal with Marsala)

---

4 veal escalopes, pounded thin
45 ml/3 tablespoons lemon juice
25 g/1 oz flour
65 g/2½ oz butter
125 ml/4 fl oz Marsala

1. Sprinkle the veal with 30 ml/2 tablespoons of the lemon juice and leave for 30 minutes. Pat dry with paper towels.

2. Season the flour, then use all but 10 ml/2 teaspoons of the flour to coat the veal.

3. Melt 50 g/2 oz of the butter in a frying pan. Add the veal and fry for about 4 minutes on each side or until lightly browned. Add the Marsala and remaining lemon juice and continue cooking for 2 minutes.

4. Mix the remaining butter with the reserved flour. Add to the liquid in the pan in small pieces and stir until thickened. Serve hot.

Serves 4

Scaloppine al Limone

(Veal with lemon sauce)

---

4 veal escalopes, pounded thin
60 ml/4 tablespoons lemon juice
65 g/2½ oz butter
175 ml/6 fl oz dry white wine
10 ml/2 teaspoons flour
Garnish
lemon slices
chopped parsley

1. Sprinkle the veal with 30 ml/2 tablespoons of the lemon juice and leave for 30 minutes. Pat dry with paper towels.

2. Melt 50 g/2 oz of the butter in a frying pan. Add the veal and fry for about 4 minutes on each side or until lightly browned. Remove the veal from the pan and keep hot.

3. Stir the wine and remaining lemon juice into the sediment in the pan and bring to the boil. Boil for 5 minutes to reduce.

4. Mix the remaining butter with the flour and add to the liquid in the pan in small pieces. Stir until thickened. Add seasoning to taste, then return the veal to the pan. Spoon the sauce over the veal and reheat for 1 minute.

5. Serve garnished with lemon slices and parsley.

Serves 4

Saltimbocca

(Veal with prosciutto and sage)

---

4 veal escalopes, pounded thin
30 ml/2 tablespoons lemon juice
10 ml/2 teaspoons chopped fresh sage or 5 ml/1 teaspoon dried sage
4 thin slices of prosciutto
50 g/2 oz butter
50 ml/2 fl oz dry white wine

1. Sprinkle the veal with the lemon juice and leave for 30 minutes. Pat dry with paper towels, then rub the veal with half the sage and seasoning to taste. Put a slice of prosciutto on each piece of veal and secure them together with wooden tooth picks.

2. Melt the butter in a frying pan. Add the remaining sage and stir well into the butter. Add the veal and fry for about 4 minutes on each side.

3. Pour over the wine and cook for a further 2–3 minutes.

4. Remove the tooth picks and serve.

Serves 4

(Top) Scaloppine al Limone *(Veal with lemon sauce) – recipe page 39*
(Bottom) Saltimbocca *(Veal with prosciutto and sage)*

Bollito Misto

(Boiled beef, chicken and sausage)

---

1 veal knuckle
1 × 2 kg/4 lb stewing chicken
1 × 700 g/1½ lb top round of beef
6 peppercorns
2 bay leaves
10 ml/2 teaspoons dried basil
2 leeks, chopped
2 celery stalks, chopped
5 carrots, sliced
12 pickling onions
1 small head of white cabbage, quartered and cored
1 kg/2 lb potatoes, peeled and sliced
1 Italian boiling sausage

1. Put the veal in a large saucepan. Half fill the pan with salted water and bring to a boil, skimming off the scum that rises to the surface. Simmer for 45 minutes. Add the chicken, beef, peppercorns and herbs to the pan. Return to the boil, then cover and simmer for 1½ hours.

2. Add the vegetables and sausage to the pan. Pour in enough water so that the vegetables are nearly covered. Stir well, then continue simmering, uncovered, for a further 1 hour or until all the meats and vegetables are cooked and tender.

3. Discard the veal. Remove the chicken, beef and sausage from the pan. Cut up the chicken, slice the beef and cut the sausage into chunks. Arrange the meats on a warmed platter.

4. Remove the vegetables from the pan with a slotted spoon and arrange them around the meats. Moisten with a few spoonsful of the stock. Use the remaining stock for soup.

Serves 8–10

Fegato alla Veneziana

(Liver with onions)

---

90 ml/6 tablespoons olive oil
3 onions, thinly sliced
450 g/1 lb calf's liver, thinly sliced and cut into 2.5 × 4 cm/1 × 1½ in
strips
lemon quarters to serve

1. Heat the oil in a frying pan. Add the onions and seasoning to taste and stir to mix with the oil. Cover the pan and cook gently for about 30 minutes or until the onions are limp and browned. Stir occasionally. Remove the onions from the pan with a slotted spoon and keep hot.

2. Put the liver strips in the pan and fry briskly for about 1 minute on each side or until they change colour.

3. Return the onions to the pan and stir to mix with the liver. Cook for a further 1 minute. Serve with lemon quarters.

Serves 4

Pollo con Peperoni

(Chicken with green pepper)

---

1 large green pepper, halved and seeded
450 g/1 lb canned tomatoes, chopped with their juice
1 onion, thinly sliced
1 garlic clove, crushed
1 chicken stock cube
8 large chicken pieces
12 black olives, stoned

1. Place the pepper halves in the grill pan, cut sides down, and grill until the skins are blistered and lightly charred. Peel off the skins, remove the cores and cut the peppers into 12 mm/$\frac{1}{2}$ in wide strips. Alternatively, if you have a gas stove, spear the whole pepper on a long-handled fork and turn it over the flame to char the skin.

2. Put the pepper strips into a saucepan and add the tomatoes, onion and garlic. Crumble in the stock cube and bring to the boil, stirring.

3. Rub the chicken pieces with seasoning and place them in the pan, skin side down. Spoon the sauce over them. Cover tightly and simmer gently for 30–40 minutes, basting occasionally.

4. Lift the chicken pieces on to a warmed serving plate and keep hot. Stir the olives into the sauce, and taste and adjust the seasoning. Pour the sauce over the chicken.

Serves 4

(Top) Pollo con Peperoni *(Chicken with green pepper)*
(Bottom) Pollo alla Milanese *(Chicken with ham and cheese)*

Pollo alla Milanese

(Chicken with ham and cheese)

---

4 chicken breasts, skinned and boned
4 slices of ham
2 tomatoes, skinned and sliced
40 g/1½ oz Parmesan cheese, grated
Marinade
30 ml/2 tablespoons oil
30 ml/2 tablespoons lemon juice

1. Place the chicken breasts between two sheets of greaseproof paper and pound with a rolling pin or meat mallet until they are flattened.

2. Arrange the chicken breasts, in one layer, in a baking dish. Mix together the ingredients for the marinade and pour over the chicken. Turn them to coat, then marinate in the refrigerator for 2 hours.

3. Preheat the oven to 150°C/300°F (Gas 2). Place a slice of ham on each chicken breast and cover with tomato slices. Sprinkle with half the cheese.

4. Cover the dish with foil and bake for 40 minutes. Uncover and sprinkle over the remaining cheese. Increase the oven temperature to 230°C/450°F (Gas 8) and move the dish to the top of the oven. Continue cooking until the cheese on top is lightly browned.

Serves 4

Petti di Pollo alla Valdostana

(Chicken breasts with mushrooms and cheese)

---

4 chicken breasts, boned
45 ml/3 tablespoons flour
65 g/2½ oz butter
50 ml/2 fl oz olive oil
125 g/4 oz tiny button mushrooms, thinly sliced
225 g/½ lb mozzarella cheese, thinly sliced
125 ml/4 fl oz white wine
75 ml/3 fl oz chicken stock

1. Place the chicken breasts between two sheets of greaseproof paper and pound with a rolling pin or meat mallet until they are flattened. Coat the chicken breasts with the flour.

2. Melt 50 g/2 oz of the butter with the oil in a frying pan. Add the chicken breasts and fry for 3–4 minutes on each side or until browned and cooked through. Transfer the chicken breasts to a warmed, flameproof serving dish. Sprinkle them with salt and pepper and keep hot. Preheat the grill.

3. Add the mushrooms to the pan and cook for 2 minutes or until barely tender. Spread the mushrooms over the chicken breasts, then cover with the cheese slices.

4. Pour the wine and stock into the pan and bring to the boil, stirring well. Simmer for 10 minutes or until the liquid becomes slightly syrupy.

5. Meanwhile, place the chicken under the grill and cook until the cheese melts and begins to brown.

6. Season the sauce in the pan and stir in the remaining butter. Pour the sauce around the chicken in the dish and serve.

Serves 4

Pollo alla Cacciatora

(Chicken with wine, tomatoes and mushrooms)

20 ml/1½ tablespoons butter
30 ml/2 tablespoons olive oil
2 garlic cloves, crushed
2 spring onions, finely chopped
175 g/6 oz mushrooms, sliced
8 chicken pieces
175 ml/6 fl oz dry white wine
50 ml/2 fl oz chicken stock
6 tomatoes, skinned, seeded and chopped
1 bay leaf
2.5 ml/½ teaspoon flour
chopped parsley to garnish

1. Melt 15 ml/1 tablespoon of the butter with the oil in a saucepan and fry the garlic and spring onions until softened. Stir in the mushrooms and fry for a further 2 minutes. Remove the vegetables from the pan with a slotted spoon.

2. Add the chicken pieces to the pan and brown on all sides. Return the vegetables to the pan and add the wine, stock, tomatoes, bay leaf and seasoning to taste. Bring to the boil, then cover and simmer for 40 minutes or until the chicken is cooked.

3. Lift out the chicken pieces and keep them hot on a serving plate. Boil the sauce to reduce it slightly.

4. Mix the remaining butter with the flour and add to the sauce in small pieces. Stir until thickened. Discard the bay leaf, and taste and adjust the seasoning. Pour the sauce over the chicken and sprinkle with chopped parsley.

Serves 4

FISH & VEGETABLES

Trote Marinate

(Trout marinated in vermouth)

---

6 small trout, cleaned
25 g/1 oz flour
60–90 ml/4–6 tablespoons oil
Marinade
125 ml/4 fl oz oil
2 onions, sliced
2 garlic cloves, sliced
45 ml/3 tablespoons white wine vinegar
75 ml/3 fl oz dry vermouth
2 strips of lemon rind
2–3 sage leaves
1 rosemary sprig
8 peppercorns

1. Coat the trout with the flour. Heat the oil in a frying pan and fry the trout, in batches, for about 5 minutes on each side or until they are golden and just cooked through. Remove from the pan and arrange, in one layer, in an earthenware dish.

2. For the marinade, heat the oil in a saucepan and fry the onions and garlic until softened. Stir in the remaining marinade ingredients and bring to the boil.

3. Pour the boiling marinade over the trout and cool. Marinate in the refrigerator for at least 3 days, turning the trout from time to time.

Serves 6

Cacciucco

(Seafood stew)

---

125 ml/4 fl oz olive oil
2 garlic cloves, chopped
1 fresh red chilli pepper, seeded and chopped
350 g/12 oz shrimps, shelled, deveined and chopped
225 g/½ lb squid, skinned, cleaned and chopped
125 ml/4 fl oz dry white wine
45 ml/3 tablespoons tomato purée
450 ml/¾ pint water
225 g/½ lb cod fillets, chopped
225 g/½ lb haddock fillets, chopped
To serve
4 slices of Italian bread, toasted
1 garlic clove, halved
30 ml/2 tablespoons chopped canned pimiento

1. Heat the oil in a saucepan and fry the garlic and chilli pepper for 5 minutes. Stir in the shrimps and squid. Cover and cook gently for 30 minutes. Stir in the wine and continue cooking, uncovered, for 15 minutes.

2. Add the tomato purée, water and seasoning to taste, and stir well. Bring to the boil. Add the cod and haddock pieces. Cover the pan again and simmer for 15 minutes.

3. Rub the bread slices on both sides with the garlic halves, then discard the garlic. Place a slice of bread in each of four soup bowls.

4. Ladle the stew over the bread and garnish with the pimiento.

Serves 4

Insalata di Mare

(Seafood salad)

---

90 ml/6 tablespoons olive oil
3 dozen mussels, scrubbed
450 ml/¾ pint water
8–10 baby squid, tentacles cut from the bodies
1.25 kg/2½ lb prawns
15 ml/1 tablespoon lemon juice
½ dried red chilli pepper, finely flaked
30 ml/2 tablespoons chopped parsley

1. Heat 30 ml/2 tablespoons of the oil in a saucepan. Add the mussels and cover tightly. Shake the mussels over the heat until they open. Remove the mussels from their shells, reserving the liquid, and place them in a shallow serving dish. Discard any where the shells do not open.

2. Put the mussel liquid back into the saucepan and add the water and squid pieces. Bring to the boil and simmer for about 20 minutes or until the squid are tender (this varies according to their size). Add the prawns and cook for 10 minutes longer.

3. Drain the squid and prawns and cool. Cut the squid bodies into rings and add with the tentacles to the mussels. Shell and devein the prawns and add to the mussels.

4. Mix the remaining olive oil with the lemon juice, chilli pepper and a pinch of salt. Stir this dressing into the seafood. Sprinkle the parsley and a little pepper on top and chill for 2 hours before serving.

Serves 6

Fritto Misto di Mare

(Deep-fried fish and shellfish)

---

oil for deep frying
2 plaice fillets, skinned and cut into strips
2 white fish fillets, skinned and cut into strips
4 scallops
350 g/12 oz Dublin Bay prawns, shelled (but tails left on) and deveined
lemon wedges to serve
parsley sprigs to garnish
Batter
125 g/4 oz flour
1.5 ml/¼ teaspoon salt
1 egg, separated
15 ml/1 tablespoon oil
250 ml/8 fl oz milk
1 egg white

1. First make the batter. Sift the flour and salt into a bowl. Add the egg yolk and oil and mix well. Gradually beat in the milk to make a smooth batter. Beat the 2 egg whites until stiff and fold into the batter.

2. Heat the oil in a deep-frying pan.

3. Coat the pieces of fish with the batter and deep fry, in batches, for 3–4 minutes or until crisp and golden brown. Drain on paper towels.

4. Serve hot with lemon wedges, garnished with parsley sprigs.

Serves 4–6

Peperonata

(Red peppers with tomatoes)

---

30 ml/2 tablespoons butter
30 ml/2 tablespoons olive oil
1 large onion, sliced
1 garlic clove, crushed
450 g/1 lb red peppers, seeded and cut into strips
450 g/1 lb tomatoes, skinned and chopped
1 bay leaf

1. Melt the butter with the oil in a saucepan and fry the onion and garlic until softened. Stir in the peppers. Cover the pan and cook gently for 15 minutes.

2. Add the tomatoes, bay leaf and seasoning to taste and mix well. Continue cooking, uncovered, for a further 20 minutes. Discard the bay leaf before serving, hot or cold.

Serves 4–6

DESSERTS

Zuccotto

(Cream and cake dessert)

---

600 ml/1 pint whipping cream
25 g/1 oz + 30 ml/2 tablespoons icing sugar, sifted
75 g/3 oz hazelnuts, toasted
225 g/¼ lb fresh cherries, halved and stoned
125 g/4 oz dark sweet chocolate, grated
50 ml/2 fl oz brandy
50 ml/2 fl oz orange liqueur
2 × 20 cm/8 in chocolate cake layers, each sliced into 2 layers
30 ml/2 tablespoons unsweetened cocoa powder

1. Whip the cream with the 25 g/1 oz sugar until thick. Fold in the hazelnuts, cherries and chocolate. Chill.

2. Mix together the brandy and liqueur.

3. Line the bottom and sides of a 900 ml/1½ pint capacity round deep mould with three of the cake layers, cutting the cake into pieces so it will fit. Sprinkle the cake with the brandy mixture.

4. Spoon the cream mixture into the cake-lined mould and cover with the remaining cake layer. Chill for 2 hours.

5. Unmould the dessert on to a serving plate. Mark it into quarters and sprinkle alternate quarters with the remaining sugar and the cocoa powder.

Serves 8–10

Ciliege al Marsala

(Cherries in Marsala)

---

1 kg/2 lb canned Morello cherries, drained and stoned
150 ml/¼ pint Marsala
2.5 ml/½ teaspoon grated nutmeg
15 ml/1 tablespoon sugar
whipped cream to serve

1. Put the cherries, Marsala, nutmeg and sugar into a saucepan and bring to the boil, stirring to dissolve the sugar. Simmer gently for 10 minutes.

2. Lift out the cherries with a slotted spoon and pile them in a serving bowl.

3. Boil the Marsala for 3–4 minutes to reduce, then pour over the cherries. Cool and chill for 1 hour. Serve topped with whipped cream.

Serves 4

Zuppa Inglese

(English 'soup' or trifle)

125 g/4 oz glacé fruit, chopped if necessary
30 ml/2 tablespoons brandy
45 ml/3 tablespoons cornflour
150 g/5 oz sugar
400 ml/14 fl oz milk
6 egg yolks, lightly beaten
5 ml/1 teaspoon vanilla essence
250 ml/8 fl oz whipped cream
125 ml/4 fl oz rum
2 × 18 cm/7 in white cake layers, each sliced into 2 layers
3 egg whites
175 g/6 oz caster sugar

1. Mix the fruit with the brandy and leave for 1 hour. Put the cornflour and sugar into a saucepan and stir in 350 ml/12 fl oz of the milk. Cook gently, stirring, until thick and smooth.

2. Mix together the egg yolks and remaining milk. Gradually stir in the thickened custard, then return to the pan. Cook gently, stirring, until very thick. Stir in the vanilla. Cool, then chill for 1 hour. Preheat the oven to 230°C/450°F (Gas 8). Fold the cream into the custard.

3. Sprinkle the rum over the cake layers. Sandwich together the layers with the custard and place the assembled cake on a greased baking sheet. Spread over the fruit and brandy mixture.

4. Beat the egg whites until frothy, then gradually beat in the sugar. Continue beating until the meringue will stand in a stiff peak. Spread over the top and sides of the cake to cover. Bake for 4–5 minutes or until the meringue is lightly browned. Cool before serving.

Serves 6

123

Cassata alla Siciliana

(Ice cream mould)

---

600 ml/1 pint vanilla ice cream, softened
300 ml/½ pint chocolate ice cream, softened
150 ml/¼ pint whipping cream
50 g/2 oz icing sugar
125 g/4 oz mixed glacé fruits, finely chopped
1 egg white

1. Use a metal spoon dipped in hot water to spread the vanilla ice cream over the bottom and sides of a 1.2 litre/2 pint freezerproof mould. Freeze until solid.

2. Cover the vanilla ice cream with a layer of chocolate ice cream, leaving a well in the centre for the filling. Freeze again until solid.

3. Whip the cream with the sugar until thick. Fold in the fruit. Beat the egg white until stiff and fold into the cream mixture. Spoon this filling into the well in the ice cream-lined mould. Tap the mould to release any air bubbles. Smooth the top and cover with foil. Freeze until firm.

4. Dip the mould quickly into hot water and unmould the cassata on to a plate. Serve cut into wedges.

Serves 8

Zabaione

(Zabaglione)

---

4 egg yolks
50 g/2 oz sugar
125 ml/4 fl oz Marsala

1. Put the egg yolks and sugar in the top of a double saucepan, away from the heat, and beat until they turn thick and creamy.

2. Place over the bottom pan containing hot, just simmering water. Add the Marsala and continue beating until the mixture becomes a creamy, thick amber foam. Serve immediately.

Serves 4

Crostata di Ricotta

(Cheesecake)

---

225 g/8 oz plain flour
175 g/6 oz butter, cut into small pieces
4 egg yolks, lightly beaten
30 ml/2 tablespoons sugar
75 ml/5 tablespoons Marsala
7.5 ml/1½ teaspoons grated lemon rind
Filling
1.25 kg/2½ lb ricotta cheese
125 g/4 oz sugar
30 ml/2 tablespoons flour
2.5 ml/½ teaspoon vanilla essence
grated rind and juice of 2 lemons
45 ml/3 tablespoons raisins
30 ml/2 tablespoons slivered almonds

1. Sift the flour and some salt into a bowl and make a well in the centre. Add the butter, egg yolks, sugar, Marsala and lemon rind and combine. Knead the dough until it is smooth and will form a ball, but do not overhandle it. Chill for 1 hour.

2. Preheat the oven to 180°C/350°F (Gas 4). Roll out three-quarters of the dough and use to line a greased 23 cm/9 in springform pan.

3. For the filling, beat the cheese with the sugar, flour, vanilla, lemon rind and juice, and raisins. Spoon into the pie shell and smooth the top. Sprinkle over the almonds.

4. Roll out the remaining dough and cut it into long strips. Lay these in a lattice pattern over the filling. Bake for 1 hour or until the pastry is golden brown and the filling is firm to the touch. Cool before serving.

Serves 6–8

MEXICAN COOKING

CONTENTS

SOUPS & STARTERS

Caldo Tlalpeno

(Chicken and bean soup)

---

1 × 2.3 kg/5 lb boiling chicken
2 onions
1 carrot, sliced
6 black peppercorns
1 bouquet garni
1.3 litres/2¼ pints water
2 green peppers, cored, seeded and sliced
450 g/1 lb canned chick peas, drained
225 g/½ lb Cheddar cheese, cubed
1 avocado, peeled, stoned and sliced

1. Put the chicken in a large saucepan. Quarter one of the onions and add to the pan with the carrot, peppercorns, bouquet garni, water, and some salt. Bring to the boil, then simmer gently for 2 hours or until the chicken is cooked through and tender. Transfer the chicken to a chopping board and cover to keep hot.

2. Boil the cooking liquid for 15 minutes. Strain the liquid and return it to the pan. Bring back to the boil.

3. Slice the remaining onion and add to the pan with the green peppers. Simmer for 10 minutes. Stir in the chick peas and simmer for a further 5 minutes.

4. Meanwhile, cut up the chicken. Return the chicken pieces to the pan and season to taste with salt and pepper. Simmer for 5 minutes to reheat. Stir in the cheese. As soon as it melts, transfer the soup to a tureen and add the avocado.

Serves 6–8

Pozole

(Thick hominy soup)

---

450 g/1 lb pork tenderloin, cubed
1 onion, sliced
1 large garlic clove, crushed
1.4 litres/2½ pints water
1 chicken breast, boned and chopped
550 g/1¼ lb canned hominy
To garnish
125 g/4 oz sliced radishes
½ crisp lettuce, shredded
4 spring onions, chopped
1 avocado, peeled, stoned and sliced
3 small limes or lemons, halved

1. Put the pork cubes, onion, garlic and water into a large saucepan and bring to the boil, skimming off any scum that rises to the surface. Cover and simmer gently for 20 minutes.

2. Add the chicken to the pan and season to taste with salt and pepper. Re-cover and simmer for a further 30 minutes.

3. Remove the pork cubes and chicken with a slotted spoon. Strain the cooking liquid and return it to the pan. Return the pork cubes and chicken to the pan and stir in the hominy. Bring to the boil and simmer for 15 minutes or until the meats are tender and the soup is thick.

4. Arrange the garnishes in separate bowls. Serve the pozole with the garnishes sprinkled on top.

Serves 6

Sopa de Aguacate

(Avocado soup)

---

2 large ripe avocados, peeled, stoned and chopped
250 ml/8 fl oz whipping cream
350 ml/12 fl oz chicken stock
5 ml/1 teaspoon lime juice
1.25 ml/¼ teaspoon crushed red chilli pepper
chopped chives or spring onions to garnish

1. Put the avocados, cream, stock, lime juice, and red chilli pepper in a blender goblet and blend until smooth. Add salt and pepper to taste.

2. Pour the soup into a bowl and chill for 2 hours.

3. Serve garnished with chives or spring onions.

Serves 4

Guacamole Ring

3 large, ripe avocados, halved and stoned
45 ml/3 tablespoons mayonnaise
juice of 1 lemon
5 ml/1 teaspoon prepared French mustard
10 ml/2 teaspoons Worcestershire sauce
30 ml/2 tablespoons tomato purée
2.5 ml/½ teaspoon each salt and pepper
300 ml/10 fl oz double cream
30 g/1 oz gelatine dissolved in 60 ml/4 tablespoons warm water
5 ml/1 teaspoon vegetable oil
Filling
450 g/1 lb prawns or shrimps, shelled
1 medium green pepper, seeded and thinly sliced
2 small red peppers, seeded and thinly sliced
30 ml/2 tablespoons fresh lemon juice
30 ml/2 tablespoons freshly chopped chives

1. Scoop the avocado flesh out of the skins and mash with the back of a wooden spoon in a medium-sized mixing bowl. Stir in the mayonnaise, lemon juice, mustard, Worcestershire sauce, tomato purée, salt and pepper. Set aside.

2. Beat the cream in a small mixing bowl until it forms soft peaks. Stir cream into the avocado mixture.

3. Stir in the dissolved gelatine. Combine mixture and spoon into a 23 cm 9-inch ring mould that has been greased with vegetable oil. Place mould in refrigerator for at least 4 hours.

4. Fifteen minutes before the mould is ready, make the filling. Combine the prawns, peppers, lemon juice and chives. Set aside.

5. Unmould the avocado mixture onto a chilled platter. Pile the prawn and pepper mixture inside the ring and arrange the remainder around the sides. Serve immediately.

Serves 8–10

Chile con Queso

(Cheese and chilli dip)

---

25 g/1 oz butter
1 onion, finely chopped or shredded
225 g/8 oz canned tomatoes, chopped with their juice
125 g/4 oz canned green chilli peppers, drained, seeded and chopped
350 g/12 oz Cheddar cheese, grated
125 ml/4 fl oz soured or double cream

1. Melt the butter in a frying pan. Add the onion and fry until softened. Stir in the tomatoes with their juice and the chilli peppers and bring to the boil. Simmer gently for 10–15 minutes or until thickened.

2. Gradually stir in the cheese and cook gently until it has melted and the mixture is smooth. Stir in the cream. If the dip is too thick, dilute it with a little milk.

3. Keep the dip warm and serve with potato crisps.

Serves 8–10

Empanadas

(Meat-filled turnovers)

---

25 g/1 oz butter
1 medium onion, finely chopped
2 tomatoes, skinned, seeded and chopped
1 small green pepper, cored, seeded and chopped
225 g/½ lb minced beef
50 g/2 oz sultanas
1 small dried red chilli pepper, crumbled
2.5 ml/½ teaspoon ground cumin
450 g/1 lb frozen puff pastry, thawed

1. Melt the butter in a frying pan. Add the onion, tomatoes and green pepper and fry until the onion is softened. Add the beef and fry until it is browned and crumbly.

2. Stir in the sultanas, chilli pepper, cumin and salt and pepper to taste. Cook gently for 10 minutes, stirring occasionally. Remove from the heat and allow to cool.

3. Preheat the oven to 190°C/375°F (Gas 5). Roll out the pastry on a lightly floured surface into a large square. Cut into eight 12.5 cm/5 in rounds.

4. Divide the beef filling between the rounds, placing it on one half of each round. Dampen the edges and fold over the rounds. Press the edges together to seal.

5. Arrange the turnovers on a greased baking sheet. Bake for 35 minutes or until the pastry is golden brown. Serve hot.

Serves 4

Ceviche

(Mackerel fillets marinated in lemon juice)

---

450 ml/¾ pint fresh lemon juice
1 small dried red chilli pepper, crumbled
2 large onions, thinly sliced into rings
½ garlic clove, chopped
3 large mackerel, filleted and cut into 2.5 cm/1 in pieces
3 large sweet potatoes
4 corn on the cob, trimmed, silks removed and cut across into 5 cm/2 in pieces
1 crisp lettuce, separated into leaves
1 fresh red chilli pepper, seeded and thinly sliced

1. Mix together the lemon juice, dried chilli pepper, onions, garlic, and salt and pepper in a shallow dish. Add the mackerel and turn to coat well. Add more lemon juice if the fish is not completely covered. Cover the dish and marinate in the refrigerator for at least 3 hours or until the fish is opaque and white.

2. About 30 minutes before serving, cook the sweet potatoes in boiling water for 30–35 minutes or until tender. Drain and peel them. Cut each one into three slices and keep hot.

3. Cook the corn in boiling water for 4–5 minutes or until just tender. Drain and keep hot.

4. Make a bed of lettuce on four serving plates. Divide the marinated fish between the plates and garnish with the marinated onion rings and strips of fresh chilli pepper. Arrange the sweet potato slices and sweetcorn around the fish and serve.

Serves 4

TORTILLAS & SAUCES

Tortillas

(Flat corn bread)

---

225 g/8 oz masa harina (cornmeal flour)
350 ml/12 fl oz lukewarm water

1. Put the masa harina in a bowl and gradually beat in the water. Knead until a smooth, elastic dough is formed. Divide the dough into 12 portions. Put each portion between two sheets of greaseproof paper. Using a rolling pin, roll out each portion, between the paper, into a very thin round about 15 cm/6 in in diameter.

2. Heat an ungreased frying pan. Peel off the greaseproof paper from one side of one round and place it, paper side up, in the pan. Cook for about $1\frac{1}{2}$ minutes or until it becomes lightly speckled brown. Peel off the paper on top, turn over the tortilla and cook the other side for about $1\frac{1}{2}$ minutes or until lightly browned.

3. Wrap the tortilla in a warm towel or foil and keep hot while you cook the remaining tortillas in the same way.

Makes 12

Huevos Rancheros

(Ranch-style eggs)

---

15 ml/1 tablespoon vegetable oil
6 tortillas (see page 142)
450 ml/¾ pint Salsa de chile rojo (see page 150)
6 eggs
50 g/2 oz butter
1 avocado, peeled, stoned and thinly sliced

1. Brush a large frying pan with some of the oil and heat it. Dip a tortilla into the chilli sauce, shake off any excess and place the tortilla in the pan. Fry for 1–2 minutes on each side or until golden brown. Transfer the tortilla to a warmed serving platter and keep hot while you fry the remaining tortillas in the same way.

2. Meanwhile, fry the eggs in the butter.

3. Pour a little of the remaining chilli sauce over the tortillas and top each with a fried egg. Garnish with the avocado slices. Serve hot, with the remaining sauce served separately.

Serves 6

Tacos with Meat

vegetable oil
1 small onion, chopped
450 g/1 lb minced beef
450 ml/¾ pint Salsa de chile rojo (see page 150)
12 tortillas (see page 142), or use ready-made taco shells
To garnish
4 tomatoes, finely chopped
¼ cucumber, diced
½ crisp lettuce, shredded
125 g/4 oz Cheddar cheese, grated

1. Heat 50 ml/2 fl oz oil in a saucepan. Add the onion and fry until softened. Add the beef and fry until it is browned and crumbly. Pour off any excess fat, then stir in the sauce and bring to the boil. Simmer gently for about 40 minutes.

2. Meanwhile, pour enough oil into a frying pan to make a 1.5 cm/¾ in layer. Heat the oil. Place one tortilla in the oil and, using tongs, fold over one side, leaving a generous space for the filling. Fry until the taco is crisp. Drain on paper towels and keep hot while you shape and fry the remaining tacos. If using taco shells, heat according to packet instructions.

3. Fill each taco shell about two-thirds full with the beef mixture and top with the garnishes. Serve hot.

Serves 4

Tostadas de Carne

(Meat tostadas)

---

45 ml/3 tablespoons vegetable oil
4 tortillas (see page 142), or use ready-made tostada shells
1 recipe Frijoles refritos, kept hot (see page 180)
½ recipe Chile con carne, kept hot (see page 152)
1 crisp lettuce, shredded
125 g/4 oz Cheddar cheese, grated
1 avocado, peeled, stoned and sliced (optional)
2 tomatoes, sliced (optional)

1. Heat the oil in a frying pan. Place one tortilla in the pan and fry for 1–2 minutes on each side or until golden brown. Transfer the tortilla to a warmed serving platter and keep hot while you fry the remaining tortillas in the same way. If using tostada shells, heat them according to packet instructions.

2. Top each tortilla with a layer of refried beans, then with chile con carne. Scatter over the lettuce and cheese and top with avocado and tomato slices, if using.

Serves 4

Variation:

Tostadas are basically Mexican-style open sandwiches so almost any topping can be used according to taste. You could try the chicken filling given on page 148, topped with chilli sauce from page 150, or even Ropa vieja on page 158.

Enchiladas

(Stuffed tortillas with tomato sauce)

---

15 ml/1 tablespoon vegetable oil
18 tortillas (see page 142)
450 ml/¾ pint Salsa de chile rojo (see page 150)
45 ml/3 tablespoons grated Cheddar cheese
Filling
25 g/1 oz butter
1 onion, finely chopped
225 g/½ lb minced beef
50 g/2 oz Cheddar cheese, grated
1 small dried red chilli pepper, crumbled

1. First make the filling. Melt the butter in a frying pan, add the onion and fry until softened. Add the beef and fry until it is browned and crumbly. Remove from the heat and stir in the remaining filling ingredients. Preheat the oven to 180°C/350°F (Gas 4).

2. Brush a large frying pan with some of the oil and heat it. Dip a tortilla into the chilli sauce, shake off any excess and place the tortilla in the pan. Fry for 1–2 minutes on each side or until golden brown. Transfer the tortilla to a plate. Spoon about 15 ml/1 tablespoon of the filling into the centre and roll up. Arrange in a greased ovenproof dish, and keep hot while you fry, fill and roll the remaining tortillas in the same way.

3. When all the tortillas are in the dish, pour the remaining sauce over them and sprinkle the grated cheese on top. Bake for 15–20 minutes or until the top is browned and bubbling. Serve hot.

Serves 6

Enchiladas Verde

(Stuffed tortillas with green tomato sauce)

---

45 ml/3 tablespoons vegetable oil
1 onion, chopped
3 chicken breasts, skinned and boned
1 recipe Salsa de tomatillo verde (see page 151)
2 small dried red chilli peppers, crumbled
12 tortillas (see page 142)
45 ml/3 tablespoons grated Parmesan cheese
45 ml/3 tablespoons grated Cheddar cheese

1. Heat 30 ml/2 tablespoons of the oil in a frying pan. Add the onion and fry until softened. Add the chicken breasts and brown on all sides. Stir in the sauce and dried chilli peppers and bring to the boil. Simmer gently for 30 minutes or until the chicken is tender. Remove from the heat.

2. Remove the chicken from the pan and chop it finely or shred it. Preheat the oven to 180°C/350°F (Gas 4).

3. Brush a large frying pan with some of the remaining oil and heat it. Dip a tortilla into the sauce in the other pan, shake off any excess and place the tortilla in the oiled pan. Fry for 1–2 minutes on each side or until golden brown. Transfer the tortilla to a plate. Spoon about 15 ml/1 tablespoon of the chicken into the centre, sprinkle with a little Parmesan cheese and roll up. Arrange in a greased ovenproof dish and keep hot while you fry, fill and roll the remaining tortillas in the same way.

4. When all the tortillas are in the dish, pour the remaining sauce over them and sprinkle the Cheddar cheese on top. Bake for 15–20 minutes or until the top is browned and bubbling. Serve hot.

Serves 4

Salsa de Chile Rojo

(Red chilli sauce)

---

3 small dried red pequin *chilli peppers, crumbled*
45 ml/3 tablespoons boiling water
450 g/1 lb canned tomatoes
50 ml/2 fl oz vegetable oil
1 onion, chopped
2 garlic cloves, crushed
30 ml/2 tablespoons tomato purée
5 ml/1 teaspoon ground cumin
20 ml/1½ tablespoons wine vinegar
2.5 ml/½ teaspoon sugar

1. Put the chilli peppers and water into a blender goblet. Drain the tomatoes, reserving the can juice, and add them to the goblet. Blend until smooth.

2. Heat the oil in a saucepan. Add the onion and garlic and fry until softened. Stir in the puréed tomato and chilli mixture, the reserved tomato can juice, and the remaining ingredients. Bring to the boil, then cover and simmer gently for 10 minutes.

Makes about 600 ml/1 pint

Salsa de Tomatillo Verde

(Green tomato sauce)

---

30 ml/2 tablespoons vegetable oil
1 large onion, chopped
450 g/1 lb canned Mexican green tomatoes (tomatillos)
2 canned green chilli peppers, drained, seeded and chopped
15 ml/1 tablespoon finely chopped fresh coriander leaves
250 ml/8 fl oz chicken stock

1. Heat the oil in a saucepan. Add the onion and fry until softened. Remove from the heat.

2. Tip the onion into a blender goblet and add the tomatoes with their juice, the chilli peppers and coriander. Blend until smooth.

3. Pour the tomato and chilli mixture back into the saucepan and stir in the stock and salt and pepper to taste. Bring to the boil, then simmer gently for 5 minutes.

Makes about 750 ml/1¼ pints

MEAT & POULTRY

Chile con Carne I

(Meat with chilli sauce)

---

30 ml/2 tablespoons corn oil
4–5 onions, finely chopped
4 garlic cloves, crushed
1.4 kg/3 lb chuck steak, cut into 1 cm/½ in cubes
75 ml/5 tablespoons chilli powder
5 ml/1 teaspoon dried oregano
10 ml/2 teaspoons ground cumin
2 dashes of Tabasco sauce
45 ml/3 tablespoons tomato purée
350 ml/12 fl oz beer

1. Heat the oil in a saucepan. Add the onions and garlic and fry until softened. Add the beef cubes and brown on all sides. Stir in the remaining ingredients and bring to the boil. Cover and simmer gently for about 45 minutes.

2. Uncover the pan and continue simmering for 20–25 minutes or until the beef is tender.

3. Taste and adjust the seasoning, then serve hot with rice and red kidney beans.

Serves 8

Chile con Carne II

(Minced beef with beans)

---

60 ml/4 tablespoons vegetable oil
2 onions, chopped
1 large garlic clove, crushed
700 g/1½ lb minced beef
225 g/8 oz canned tomatoes, chopped in their juice
45 ml/3 tablespoons tomato purée
1 bay leaf
5 ml/1 teaspoon ground cumin
1.25 ml/¼ teaspoon cayenne pepper
15 ml/1 tablespoon mild chilli seasoning
250 ml/8 fl oz beef stock
400 g/14 oz canned red kidney beans, drained

1. Heat the oil in a large saucepan. Add the onions and garlic and fry until the onions are softened. Add the beef and fry until it is browned and crumbly.

2. Stir in the tomatoes with their juice, tomato purée, bay leaf, cumin, cayenne, chilli seasoning and stock, and bring to the boil. Cover and simmer for 1 hour, stirring occasionally.

3. Stir in the kidney beans, re-cover the pan and simmer for a further 15 minutes. Remove the bay leaf and serve hot.

Serves 4–6

Picadillo

(Beef with apples, sultanas and olives)

---

45 ml / 3 tablespoons vegetable oil
1 large onion, chopped
1 garlic clove, crushed
1 kg / 2 lb minced beef
450 g / 1 lb canned tomatoes, drained and chopped
30 ml / 2 tablespoons tomato purée
1 large cooking apple, peeled, cored and chopped
2 canned jalapeño *chilli peppers, drained, seeded and chopped*
50 g / 2 oz sultanas
10 pimento-stuffed green olives, sliced
2.5 ml / ½ teaspoon ground cinnamon
1.25 ml / ¼ teaspoon ground cloves
45 ml / 3 tablespoons toasted slivered almonds

1. Heat the oil in a large saucepan. Add the onion and garlic and fry until softened. Add the beef and fry until it is browned and crumbly.

2. Stir in the tomatoes, tomato purée, apple, chilli peppers, sultanas, olives, spices, and salt and pepper to taste. Bring to the boil, then simmer gently for 40 minutes.

3. Pour the mixture into a warmed serving dish and scatter over the almonds. Serve hot.

Serves 6

Mole de Olla

(Beef stew with chilli sauce)

---

50 ml/2 fl oz vegetable oil
1 kg/2 lb chuck steak, cubed
15 ml/1 tablespoon chopped fresh coriander leaves
2 potatoes, quartered
2 carrots, quartered
2 large corn on the cob, trimmed, silks removed and cut across into
5 cm/2 in pieces
Mole sauce
700 g/1½ lb canned Mexican green tomatoes (tomatillos)
1 small onion, chopped
1 garlic clove, crushed
125 g/4 oz canned green chilli peppers, drained, halved and seeded
15 ml/1 tablespoon sesame seeds
2.5 ml/½ teaspoon chilli powder
2.5 ml/½ teaspoon ground cumin

1. First make the mole sauce. Put all the ingredients into a blender goblet and blend until smooth.

2. Heat the oil in a large saucepan. Add the beef cubes, in batches, and fry until browned on all sides.

3. Stir in the mole sauce, coriander, and salt and pepper to taste. Bring to the boil, then cover and simmer gently for 1 hour.

4. Stir in the potatoes, carrots and corn. Cover again and continue simmering gently for 1 hour or until the meat is tender. Adjust the seasoning before serving.

Serves 6

RopaVieja

(Shredded beef stew)

---

1 kg/2 lb chuck steak, cut into small cubes
1 large onion, sliced
1 garlic clove, crushed
30 ml/2 tablespoons vinegar
450 ml/¾ pint water or beef stock
4 tomatoes, skinned and chopped
50 ml/2 fl oz vegetable oil
2 potatoes, cooked and sliced
1 red pepper, cored, seeded and sliced
1 green pepper, cored, seeded and sliced
1 hard-boiled egg, chopped

1. Put the beef, onion, garlic, vinegar, water or stock, and salt and pepper to taste into a large saucepan. Bring to the boil, then cover and simmer gently for 1½ hours.

2. Stir in the tomatoes and simmer, uncovered, for a further 45 minutes or until the beef is very tender.

3. Heat the oil in another large saucepan. Add the potatoes and peppers and fry until the peppers are tender. Add the beef mixture, shredding the beef slightly with a fork, and cook gently until the liquid almost evaporates.

4. Transfer to a warmed serving dish and garnish with the egg. Serve hot.

Serves 4–6

Mancha Manteles de Cerdo

(Pork tablecloth stainer)

1 kg/2 lb boned pork, cubed
2 bay leaves
2 cloves
600 ml/1 pint cold water
3 dried ancho *chilli peppers*
125 ml/4 fl oz boiling water or chicken stock
50 g/2 oz chopped walnuts
350 g/12 oz canned Mexican green tomatoes (tomatillos)
1 small onion, chopped
1 garlic clove, crushed
30 ml/2 tablespoons chopped fresh coriander leaves
2 apples, peeled, cored and sliced
2 pears, peeled, cored and sliced
175 g/6 oz canned pineapple chunks, drained
225 g/8 oz packet frozen peas

1. Put the pork, bay leaves, cloves, cold water, and salt and pepper into a large saucepan and bring to the boil. Cover and simmer for 50 minutes. Meanwhile, soak the chilli peppers in the boiling water or stock for 15 minutes.

2. Remove the pork from the pan with a slotted spoon. Strain the cooking liquid and reserve 350 ml/12 fl oz.

3. Tip the soaked chilli pepper mixture into a blender goblet and add the walnuts, tomatoes and can juice, onion, garlic, and coriander. Blend until smooth. Stir in the reserved pork liquid.

4. Return the pork to the saucepan and layer the apples, pears and pineapple on top. Pour over the chilli sauce. Bring to the boil, then cover and simmer gently for 20 minutes. Stir in the peas and simmer for a further 5 minutes. Serve hot.

Serves 6

Tinga de Cerdo y Ternera

(Pork and veal stew)

---

50 g/2 oz butter
30 ml/2 tablespoons vegetable oil
1 kg/2 lb boned pork, cubed
1 kg/2 lb stewing veal, cubed
2 onions, finely chopped
3 garlic cloves, crushed
1 kg/2 lb canned Mexican green tomatoes (tomatillos), drained and chopped
3 green peppers, cored, seeded and chopped
4 fresh green chilli peppers, seeded and chopped
30 ml/2 tablespoons tomato purée
15 ml/1 tablespoon chopped fresh marjoram
15 ml/1 tablespoon chopped chives
15 ml/1 tablespoon chopped fresh basil
10 ml/2 teaspoons grated nutmeg
5 ml/1 teaspoon sugar
250 ml/8 fl oz chicken stock
250 ml/8 fl oz dry sherry
90 ml/6 tablespoons double cream

1. Melt the butter with the oil in a large saucepan. Add the pork and veal cubes and brown on all sides. Remove them from the pan.

2. Add the onions and garlic to the pan and fry until softened. Stir in the tomatoes, green peppers, chilli peppers, tomato purée, herbs, nutmeg, sugar, and salt and pepper to taste. Cook for 5 minutes, stirring frequently.

3. Return the meat to the pan with the stock and sherry. Bring to the boil, stirring well, then cover and simmer gently for 1½ hours or until the meat is tender. Remove from the heat and stir in the cream. Serve hot.

Serves 8–10

Pork Adobo

---

450 g/1 lb canned tomatoes
30 ml/2 tablespoons vinegar
1 onion, chopped
1 garlic clove, crushed
3 dried red chilli peppers, crumbled
or 15 ml/1 tablespoon chilli powder
2.5ml/½ teaspoon dried oregano
2.5 ml/½ teaspoon cumin seeds
50 ml/2 fl oz vegetable oil
4 large pork chops
1 avocado, peeled, stoned and sliced

1. Put the tomatoes with their juice, vinegar, onion, garlic, chilli peppers or chilli powder, oregano and cumin in a blender goblet and blend until smooth.

2. Heat the oil in a large frying pan. Add the chops and brown on both sides.

3. Pour the chilli sauce over the pork chops and bring to the boil. Add salt and pepper to taste. Cover and simmer gently for 40–50 minutes or until the pork is cooked through and tender.

4. Serve garnished with the avocado slices.

Serves 4

Albondigas

(Meatball with tomato sauce)

---

2 slices of white bread
50 ml/2 fl oz milk
450 g/1 lb minced beef
225 g/½ lb minced pork
5 ml/1 teaspoon dried oregano
1 small onion, finely chopped
10 ml/2 teaspoons chilli seasoning
1 egg, lightly beaten
8 pimento-stuffed green olives, halved
Sauce
50 ml/2 fl oz vegetable oil
1 garlic clove, crushed
450 g/1 lb canned tomatoes, chopped with their juice
350 ml/12 fl oz tomato juice
2.5 ml/½ teaspoon ground cumin
few dashes of Tabasco sauce

1. Soak the bread in the milk for 10 minutes. Put the beef, pork, oregano, onion, chilli seasoning and egg in a large mixing bowl and add the soaked bread. Beat briskly until well combined.

2. Shape the meat mixture into walnut-sized balls. Push an olive half into each ball and press the meat mixture around to enclose it completely.

3. Heat the oil in a saucepan. Add the garlic and fry for 1 minute. Add the remaining sauce ingredients and stir well. Bring to the boil, then simmer for 10 minutes.

4. Carefully add the meatballs to the sauce. Cover the pan and simmer gently for 30–40 minutes or until the meatballs are cooked through. Serve hot, with rice.

Serves 6

Duck with Mole Sauce

1 × 2.5 kg/5½ lb duck with giblets
1 small carrot, finely chopped
1 small onion, finely chopped
1 garlic clove, crushed
5 black peppercorns
Mole verde
450 g/1 lb canned Mexican green tomatoes (tomatillos), drained and chopped
2 fresh green chilli peppers, seeded and chopped
1 small onion, chopped
2 garlic cloves, chopped
2 large lettuce leaves, chopped
1 small bunch of radish leaves
4 fresh coriander sprigs

1. Remove the giblets from the duck and place them in a saucepan. Add the carrot, onion, garlic, peppercorns, and 7.5 ml/1½ teaspoons salt. Cover with water. Bring to the boil, then simmer gently for 1½ hours.

2. Meanwhile, prick the duck skin all over. Heat a large saucepan, put in the duck and brown on all sides. Drain off the duck fat periodically and reserve it. Cover the pan tightly and cook gently for 1 hour or until the duck is tender.

3. Meanwhile, to make the mole verde, put all the ingredients in a blender goblet and blend until smooth. Strain the giblet stock. Return it to the pan and boil until reduced to 300 ml/½ pint.

4. Heat 30 ml/2 tablespoons of the reserved duck fat in another pan. Stir in the mole verde and pepper to taste. Simmer for 5 minutes. Stir in the reduced stock and simmer for 15 minutes.

5. Cut the duck into portions and arrange on a warmed serving platter. Pour over the sauce and serve hot.

Serves 4

Pollo in Vino Tinto

(Chicken in red wine)

---

125 ml/4 fl oz olive oil
125 ml/4 fl oz wine vinegar
1 garlic clove, crushed
1 onion, chopped
1 bouquet garni
1 bay leaf
4 chicken pieces
3 bacon rashers, rinded and chopped
2 carrots, chopped
450 g/1 lb canned tomatoes, chopped with their juice
300 ml/½ pint red wine

1. Mix together the oil, vinegar, garlic, onion, bouquet garni, bay leaf, and salt and pepper to taste in a shallow dish. Add the chicken pieces and turn to coat. Cover and leave to marinate in the refrigerator overnight.

2. The next day, fry the bacon in a large saucepan until it renders its fat. Add the carrots and fry gently for 5 minutes. Pour off any excess fat, then stir in the tomatoes and wine and bring to the boil.

3. Add the chicken with its marinade and return to the boil. Cover and simmer gently for 1 hour or until the chicken is tender. Discard the bouquet garni and bay leaf. Serve hot.

Serves 4

Mole Poblano

(Turkey with chocolate sauce)

---

75 g/3 oz lard
1 × 4.5 kg/10 lb turkey, jointed
1 large onion, finely chopped
75 g/3 oz sultanas
125 g/4 oz ground almonds
3 tomatoes, skinned and chopped
50 g/2 oz toasted sesame seeds
2 tortillas (see page 142), crumbled
5 ml/1 teaspoon ground cinnamon
3 small dried red chilli peppers, crumbled
600 ml/1 pint turkey giblet stock, strained
50 g/2 oz plain chocolate

1. Melt half the lard in a large saucepan, add the turkey pieces and brown on all sides. Add enough water to cover and bring to the boil. Cover and simmer for $1\frac{1}{2}$ hours or until tender.

2. Meanwhile, to make the sauce, melt the remaining lard in a saucepan. Add the onion and fry until softened. Stir in the sultanas, almonds, tomatoes, half the sesame seeds, the tortillas, cinnamon and chilli peppers and cook for 8 minutes, stirring.

3. Stir in half the giblet stock and bring to the boil. Remove from the heat. Stir the remaining stock into the sauce, then pour a little into a blender goblet. Blend until smooth. When all the sauce has been blended, return it to the saucepan. Add the chocolate and heat gently until melted. Cook until the sauce is smooth and thick.

4. Drain the turkey and arrange the pieces on a warmed serving platter. Pour over a little of the sauce and sprinkle over the remaining sesame seeds. Serve the rest of the sauce separately.

Serves 8–10

RICE DISHES

Mexican Rice

---

1 large onion, chopped
2 garlic cloves, chopped
450 g/1 lb canned tomatoes
2.5 ml/½ teaspoon paprika
50 ml/2 fl oz olive oil
300 g/11 oz long-grain rice
750 ml/1¼ pints chicken stock
4 fresh chilli peppers
275 g/10 oz frozen peas
1 large avocado, peeled, stoned and sliced
fresh coriander or parsley sprigs to garnish

1. Put the onion, garlic and tomatoes with their juice into a blender goblet. Blend until smooth. Stir in the paprika.

2. Heat the oil in a saucepan. Add the rice and stir until it is well coated with the oil. Add the tomato mixture and stock and bring to the boil, stirring well. Cover tightly and cook gently for 40 minutes or until the rice is tender and has absorbed the liquid. Stir from time to time.

3. Meanwhile, slice the chilli peppers from tip to stem, making about five cuts so that they open out like a flower.

4. Stir the peas and salt and pepper to taste into the rice mixture and cook, uncovered, for a further 5 minutes.

5. Spoon the rice mixture into a warmed serving dish and garnish with the chilli pepper flowers, avocado slices, and coriander or parsley sprigs.

Serves 6

Mexican Pork and Rice

30 ml/2 tablespoons vegetable oil
1 medium onion, chopped
450 g/1 lb minced pork
225 g/½ lb pork sausagemeat
2 celery sticks, cut into 2.5 cm/1 in pieces
1 small green pepper, cored, seeded and cut into rings
75 g/3 oz sultanas
1 garlic clove, crushed
2.5 ml/¼ teaspoon ground cumin
1 small dried red chilli pepper, crumbled
200 g/7 oz long-grain rice
450 g/1 lb canned tomatoes
125 ml/4 fl oz water
30 ml/2 tablespoons tomato purée
juice of ½ lemon
45 ml/3 tablespoons pine nuts

1. Preheat the oven to 180°C/350°F (Gas 4). Heat the oil in a flameproof casserole. Add the onion and fry until softened. Stir in the pork and sausagemeat and fry until no longer pink.

2. Stir in the celery, green pepper, sultanas, garlic, cumin, chilli pepper, rice, and salt and pepper to taste. Fry for 5 minutes, stirring constantly. Stir in the tomatoes with their juice, the water, and tomato purée. Bring to the boil, then cover and simmer for 10 minutes.

3. Transfer the casserole to the oven and bake for 25 minutes.

4. Sprinkle the lemon juice and pine nuts over the rice mixture. Return to the oven and bake, uncovered, for a further 10 minutes. Serve hot, from the casserole.

Serves 4–6

Shellfish with Rice

50 ml/2 fl oz vegetable oil
2 onions, chopped
1 garlic clove, crushed
400 g/14 oz long-grain rice
450 ml/¾ pint water
450 g/1 lb canned tomatoes, chopped with their juice
30 ml/2 tablespoons tomato purée
5 ml/1 teaspoon powdered saffron
2 small dried red chilli peppers, crumbled
8–10 clams
225 g/8 oz peeled shrimps
225 g/8 oz cooked crabmeat, flaked
225 g/8 oz frozen peas

1. Heat the oil in a large saucepan. Add the onions and garlic and fry until softened. Stir in the rice until well coated with the oil.

2. Add the water, tomatoes, tomato purée, saffron and chilli pepper and mix well. Bring to the boil, then cover and simmer gently for 15 minutes.

3. Meanwhile, scrub the clams thoroughly. Steam them for 8–10 minutes or until they open (discard any that do not open). Remove one shell from each clam.

4. Stir the shrimps, crabmeat and peas into the rice mixture and simmer for a further 5 minutes.

5. Add salt and pepper to taste, then arrange the clams on top. Heat through for a final 1–2 minutes, then serve.

Serves 6

Arroz con Pollo

(Chicken with saffron rice)

---

6 bacon rashers, rinded
60 ml/4 tablespoons flour
1 × 2.3 kg/5 lb chicken, jointed
2 onions, chopped
1 garlic clove, crushed
450 g/1 lb canned tomatoes
75 g/3 oz canned pimentos, drained
10 ml/2 teaspoons paprika
1.25 ml/$\frac{1}{4}$ teaspoon powdered saffron
600 ml/1 pint water
250 g/9 oz long-grain rice
275 g/10 oz frozen peas

1. Fry the bacon in a flameproof casserole until it renders its fat. Remove the bacon and drain on paper towels. Crumble and reserve.

2. Mix the flour with salt and pepper and use to coat the chicken pieces. Add the to the casserole and fry in the bacon fat until browned on all sides. Remove the chicken from the casserole. Preheat the oven to 180°C/350°F (Gas 4).

3. Add the onions and garlic to the casserole and fry until softened. Arrange the chicken pieces on the onions and pour over the tomatoes with their juice, the pimentos, paprika, saffron and water. Bring to the boil, then stir in the rice.

4. Cover the casserole and transfer it to the oven. Cook for 35 minutes. Stir in the peas and crumbled bacon and cook for a further 15–20 minutes or until the chicken is tender. Serve hot.

Serves 4–6

FISH & SEAFOOD

Huachinango Yucateco

(Red snapper Yucatan-style)

---

50 g/2 oz butter
1 medium onion, chopped
1 garlic clove, crushed
1 small red pepper, cored, seeded and chopped
1 small green pepper, cored, seeded and chopped
15 ml/1 tablespoon chopped fresh coriander leaves
5 ml/1 teaspoon ground cumin
2.5 ml/½ teaspoon grated orange rind
125 ml/4 fl oz orange juice
1 × 2.3 kg/5 lb red snapper, gurnet or sea bream, cleaned
6 black olives, stoned and chopped
1 avocado, peeled, stoned and thinly sliced

1. Melt half the butter in a saucepan. Add the onion, garlic and peppers and fry until softened. Stir in the coriander, cumin, orange rind and juice, and salt and pepper to taste. Bring to the boil and simmer for 2 minutes. Remove from the heat.

2. Preheat the oven to 180°C/350°F (Gas 4). Cut the remaining butter into small pieces and scatter them over the bottom of a large, shallow casserole. Place the fish on top and pour over the orange and pepper mixture. Scatter over the olives.

3. Put the dish into the oven and bake for 25–30 minutes or until the fish flakes easily when tested with a fork. Baste the fish occasionally with the liquid in the dish.

4. Garnish with the avocado slices and serve hot.

Serves 6

Huachinango Veracruzano

(Red snapper Vera Cruz-style)

---

50 ml/2 fl oz vegetable oil
1 large onion, chopped
1 garlic clove, crushed
700 g/1½ lb canned tomatoes, chopped with their juice
2 small dried red chilli peppers, crumbled
6 pimento-stuffed green olives, chopped
6 black olives, stoned and chopped
40 g/1½ oz flour
700 g/1½ lb red snapper, gurnet or sea bream fillets
50 g/2 oz butter

1. Heat the oil in a saucepan. Add the onion and garlic and fry until softened. Stir in the tomatoes, chilli peppers and olives. Bring to the boil and simmer gently for 20 minutes.

3. Meanwhile, mix the flour with salt and pepper and use to coat the fish fillets. Melt the butter in a large frying pan. Add the fillets and fry for 4–6 minutes on each side or until browned and cooked through.

3. Arrange the fish on a warmed serving platter. Pour over the tomato and chilli sauce and serve.

Serves 4

Escabeche

(Pickled fish)

---

45 ml/3 tablespoons flour
700 g–1 kg/1½–2 lb white fish fillets
150 ml/¼ pint olive oil
2 large onions, sliced
1 red pepper, cored, seeded and sliced
2 garlic cloves, chopped
1 red chilli pepper, seeded and chopped
3 bay leaves
1.25 ml/¼ teaspoon black peppercorns
300 ml/½ pint red wine vinegar

1. Mix together the flour and 5 ml/1 teaspoon salt and use to coat the fish fillets.

2. Heat 90 ml/6 tablespoons of the oil in a large frying pan. Add the fish and fry for 4–5 minutes on each side or until browned and cooked through. Drain the fish on paper towels.

3. Wipe out the pan. Heat the remaining oil in it, add the onions and fry until softened. Stir in the red pepper, garlic, chilli pepper, bay leaves, peppercorns and vinegar. Bring to the boil and simmer for 2 minutes.

4. Arrange the fish in an earthenware or heatproof glass dish. Pour over the vinegar mixture and cover. Cool, then place in the refrigerator. Leave to marinate for 2–3 days.

Serves 4–6

(Top) Escabeche
(Bottom) Pipian de Camarones

Pipian de Camarones

(Shrimp with pumpkin seed sauce)

---

50 g/2 oz roasted salted pumpkin seeds
5 ml/1 teaspoon coriander seeds
1 small onion, chopped
1 garlic clove, crushed
1 dried red chilli pepper, crumbled
225 g/8 oz canned tomatoes
20 ml/1½ tablespoons chopped fresh coriander leaves
50 ml/2 fl oz vegetable oil
450 g/1 lb peeled shrimps
125 ml/4 fl oz chicken stock
30 ml/2 tablespoons lime juice

1. Put the pumpkin and coriander seeds into a blender goblet and add the onion, garlic, chilli pepper, tomatoes with their juice, and coriander leaves. Blend until smooth.

2. Heat the oil in a large frying pan. Add the shrimps and fry gently for about 3 minutes, stirring constantly. Transfer to a warmed serving dish. Keep hot.

3. Pour the pumpkin seed mixture into the frying pan and stir in the stock and lime juice. Heat, stirring, until piping hot.

4. Pour the sauce over the shrimps and serve.

Serves 4

SALADS & VEGETABLES

Ensalada de Nochebuena

(Christmas Eve salad)

---

1 lettuce, shredded
2 apples, cored and sliced
2 bananas, sliced
30 ml/2 tablespoons lemon juice
2 oranges, peeled and sliced
225 g/8 oz canned pineapple chunks, drained
4 cooked beetroots, peeled and sliced
45 ml/3 tablespoons wine vinegar
90–105 ml/6–7 tablespoons olive or sunflower oil
5 ml/1 teaspoon sugar
125 g/4 oz unsalted peanuts
50 g/2 oz pomegranate seeds

1. Make a bed of shredded lettuce on a serving platter.

2. Dip the apples and bananas in the lemon juice to prevent them discolouring, then arrange, with the oranges, pineapple chunks, and beetroot slices, on the lettuce in a decorative pattern.

3. Beat together the vinegar, oil, sugar, and salt and pepper to taste.

4. Pour this dressing over the salad and sprinkle the peanuts and pomegranate seeds on top.

Serves 6

Frijoles Refritos

(Refried beans)

---

350 g/12 oz dried kidney or pinto beans, soaked overnight and drained
1 small chorizo sausage, skinned and diced
40 g/1½ oz lard
1 onion, chopped
3 medium tomatoes, skinned, seeded and chopped
2 small dried red chilli peppers, crumbled
50 g/2 oz Cheddar cheese, grated

1. Put the beans and 2.5 ml/½ teaspoon salt into a saucepan and cover with fresh water. Bring to the boil, then cover and simmer for 1½ hours or until the beans are tender. Drain and purée them in a blender until smooth.

2. Fry the chorizo in a frying pan for 5 minutes, stirring occasionally. Do not add any fat as the sausage will render a lot of its own. Drain the sausage on paper towels. Pour off the fat from the pan.

3. Melt the lard in the pan. Add the onion and fry until softened. Stir in the tomatoes, chilli peppers and salt to taste and cook for 5 minutes or until the mixture becomes pulpy.

4. Stir in the chorizo, puréed beans, and the cheese. Cook gently, stirring frequently, for 10 minutes or until the mixture is very thick. Serve hot.

Serves 4

Chiles Rellenos I

(Stuffed green chilli peppers)

---

400 g/14 oz canned Californian green chilli peppers, drained
175 g/6 oz Cheddar cheese, cut into strips to fit the chilli peppers
50 g/2 oz flour
3 eggs, separated
15 ml/1 tablespoon water
45 ml/3 tablespoons cornflour
vegetable oil for deep frying
350 ml/12 fl oz Salsa de chile rojo, kept hot (see page 150)

1. Cut a slit down one side of each chilli pepper and remove any seeds and membrane. Rinse under running water, then pat dry with paper towels. Stuff with the cheese strips.

2. Mix the flour with salt and pepper and use to coat the stuffed chilli peppers.

3. Beat together the egg yolks, water and cornflour until smooth. Whisk the egg whites until stiff and fold into the yolk mixture to make a batter.

4. Heat oil in a deep fat fryer to 182°C/360°F. Dip the chilli peppers into the batter to coat well, then drop into the oil. Fry for 3–4 minutes or until puffed up and lightly browned. Drain on paper towels.

5. Pile the fried chilli peppers on a warmed serving plate and pour over the sauce. Serve hot.

Serves 4

Overleaf: *(Top)* Chiles Rellenos II
(Bottom) Chiles en Nogada

Chiles Rellenos II

(Stuffed peppers)

---

4 large green or red peppers
50 ml/2 fl oz olive oil
2 medium onions, finely chopped
2 small dried red chilli peppers, crumbled
450 g/1 lb minced beef
5 ml/1 teaspoon dried oregano
2.5 ml/½ teaspoon Tabasco sauce
15 g/½ oz flour
250 ml/8 fl oz beef stock
45 ml/3 tablespoons tomato purée
Sauce
225 g/8 oz full fat soft cheese
125 ml/4 fl oz single cream
1.25 ml/¼ teaspoon cayenne pepper
75 g/3 oz sultanas

1. Cut the tops from the peppers and scoop out the cores and seeds. Chop the pepper tops.

2. Heat the oil in a saucepan. Add the onions, chilli peppers and chopped pepper tops and fry until softened. Stir in the beef, oregano and Tabasco and fry until the beef is browned. Stir in the flour, stock, tomato purée and salt and pepper to taste. Cover and simmer for 30 minutes, stirring occasionally.

3. Preheat the oven to 180°C/350°F (Gas 4). Spoon the beef into the peppers. Arrange in a greased ovenproof dish and bake for 40 minutes.

4. Meanwhile, make the sauce. Put the cheese, cream, and cayenne into a saucepan and heat gently, stirring until the mixture is smooth and hot. Stir in the sultanas. Pour the sauce over the peppers and bake for a further 15 minutes. Serve hot.

Serves 4

Chiles en Nogada

(Stuffed peppers with walnut cream sauce)

4 large green peppers
30 ml/2 tablespoons vegetable oil
1 onion, finely chopped
1 garlic clove, crushed
450 g/1 lb minced beef
225 g/8 oz canned tomatoes, drained and chopped
45 ml/3 tablespoons seedless raisins
5 ml/1 teaspoon ground cinnamon
Sauce
250 ml/8 fl oz single cream
125 g/4 oz ground walnuts
15 ml/1 tablespoon ground almonds
50 g/2 oz pomegranate seeds

1. Cut the tops from the peppers and scoop out the cores and seeds. Discard the tops. Blanch the peppers in boiling water for 5 minutes. Drain and leave to dry.

2. Heat the oil in a saucepan. Add the onion and garlic and fry until softened. Add the beef and fry until it is browned.

3. Stir in the tomatoes, raisins, cinnamon, and salt and pepper. Bring to the boil, then simmer for 10 minutes until thick.

4. Preheat the oven to 180°C/350°F (Gas 4). Spoon the meat into the peppers. Arrange in a greased ovenproof dish and bake for 30 minutes.

5. Meanwhile, make the sauce. Put the cream, walnuts, almonds and salt and pepper to taste into a saucepan. Heat gently, stirring, until piping hot and thickened. Transfer the peppers to a warmed serving platter. Pour over the sauce and scatter the pomegranate seeds on top. Serve hot.

Serves 4

DESSERTS & CAKES
Huevos Reales
(Royal eggs)

---

2 eggs, separated
4 egg yolks
40 g/1½ oz seedless raisins
125 ml/4 fl oz sherry
350 g/12 oz sugar
175 ml/6 fl oz water
1 cinnamon stick

1. Preheat the oven to 170°C/325°F (Gas 3). Beat all the egg yolks together until they are very thick and will form a ribbon trail when the beater is lifted from the bowl. In another bowl, whisk the egg whites until stiff. Fold the egg whites into the egg yolks, and pour into a buttered ovenproof dish.

2. Place the dish in a roasting tin and add enough hot water to the tin to come halfway up the sides of the dish. Bake for 20 minutes or until the eggs are firm. Cool the eggs to room temperature. Meanwhile, soak the raisins in half the sherry.

3. Put the sugar, water and cinnamon stick into a small saucepan and heat, stirring to dissolve the sugar. Bring to the boil and boil briskly without stirring until the syrup thickens. Remove from the heat. Discard the cinnamon stick.

4. Cut the eggs into small squares and loosen them in the dish. Pour over the syrup and turn the squares over to coat on all sides. Sprinkle over the soaked raisins and the remaining sherry and serve.

Serves 4

Capirotada

(Bread pudding)

---

250 ml/8 fl oz water
225 g/8 oz dark brown sugar
7.5 ml/1½ teaspoons ground cinnamon
50 g/2 oz butter
10 slices of stale bread, crusts removed and cubed
50 g/2 oz sultanas
125 g/4 oz chopped walnuts
175 g/6 oz cottage cheese

1. Preheat the oven to 190°C/375°F (Gas 5). Put the water, sugar and half the cinnamon into a sucepan and heat, stirring to dissolve the sugar. Simmer without stirring for 5 minutes.

2. Meanwhile, melt the butter in a frying pan. Add the bread cubes and fry until browned on all sides. Stir the bread cubes into the syrup with the sultanas, walnuts and cheese.

3. Pour the bread cube mixture into a greased ovenproof dish. Sprinkle over the remaining cinnamon. Bake for 15–20 minutes or until the pudding has set and is golden brown. Serve with whipped cream.

Serves 4

Almendrado

(Almond pudding with custard sauce)

---

225 g/8 oz + 30 ml/2 tablespoons sugar
7.5 ml/1½ teaspoons gelatine
300 ml/½ pint water
5 eggs, separated
2.5 ml/½ teaspoon almond extract
red and green food colouring
50 g/2 oz slivered almonds
300 ml/½ pint milk

1. Put 225 g/8 oz of the sugar in a saucepan with the gelatine and water. Cook, stirring, until the gelatine dissolves. Cool, then chill until the mixture is like unbeaten egg white.

2. Tip the gelatine mixture into a mixing bowl. Add the egg whites and almond extract. Beat for about 5 minutes or until light. Remove 150 ml/¼ pint of the mixture and tint it pink with red food colouring. Spoon into a 1.4 litre/2½ pint pudding basin or mould and chill for 15 minutes.

3. Divide the remaining beaten mixture in half. Tint one half green with food colouring and fold the almonds into the other half. Spoon the almond mixture into the mould over the pink layer and chill for 15 minutes. Spread the green mixture over the almond mixture and chill for several hours.

4. Meanwhile, put the egg yolks, remaining sugar and milk in a heavy-based saucepan and heat gently, stirring, until the custard coats the back of the spoon. Remove from the heat. Cover sauce with dampened greaseproof paper and chill.

5. Unmould the pudding on to a serving platter. Serve with the custard sauce.

Serves 8

Rosca de Reyes

15 g/½ oz yeast
75 g/3 oz sugar
45 ml/3 tablespoons lukewarm water
450 g/1 lb flour
175 ml/6 fl oz milk, scalded
60 g/2½ oz butter, melted
2 eggs, lightly beaten
30 ml/2 tablespoons cinnamon sugar
225 g/8 oz chopped mixed peel
125 t/4 oz icing sugar
2.5 ml/½ teaspoon vanilla flavouring

1. Mix the yeast with 5 ml/1 teaspoon of the sugar and the water. Leave in a warm place until frothy. Sift the four and salt into a mixing bowl. In another bowl, mix the remaining sugar with the milk and melted butter until dissolved.

2. Add the yeast and milk mixtures to the flour with the eggs and beat to form a dough. Tip on to a floured surface and knead for 10 minutes or until elastic. Shape into a ball and place in a greased polythene bag. Leave to rise for 1½ hours.

3. Punch down the dough and knead for 3 minutes. Roll out into a 51 × 25.5 cm/20 × 10 in rectangle. Sprinkle over the cinnamon sugar and chopped peel.

4. Starting from a long edge, roll up like a Swiss roll. Place, seam down, in a ring on a greased baking sheet. Cover and leave to rise for 45 minutes. Preheat the oven to 190°C/375°F (Gas 5). Bake the bread for 25–30 minutes or until cooked through. Cool on a wire rack.

5. Sift the icing sugar into a bowl and stir in the vanilla and enough water to make a spreading icing. Spread over the bread and leave to set before serving.

Churros

(Fried choux pastries)

---

150 ml/¼ pint water
40 g/1½ oz butter, cut into small pieces
2.5 ml/½ teaspoon salt
pinch of grated nutmeg
150 g/5 oz flour, sifted
3 eggs
vegetable oil for deep frying
sifted icing sugar

1. Put the water, butter, salt and nutmeg in a saucepan and bring to the boil, stirring to melt the butter. Remove the pan from the heat and beat in the flour all at once. Continue beating until the mixture pulls away from the sides of the pan.

2. Beat in the eggs, one at a time. When all the eggs have been absorbed, the dough should be thick and glossy. Cool.

3. Spoon the dough into a piping bag fitted with a 1 cm/½ in plain nozzle. Heat oil in a deep fat fryer to 180°C/350°F.

4. Pipe 20.5 cm/8 in lengths of dough into the oil, cutting the lengths with scissors. Deep fry for about 8 minutes or until crisp and golden brown. Drain on paper towels.

5. Sprinkle with icing sugar and serve hot or cold.

Serves 4

GERMAN
COOKING

CONTENTS

SOUPS & STARTERS

Linsensuppe

(Lentil and vegetable soup)

---

450 g/1 lb lentils, soaked overnight and drained
2.3 litres/4 pints boiling water
225 g/½ lb piece of lean bacon
1 leek, chopped
2 large carrots, peeled and chopped
2 celery sticks, chopped
30 ml/2 tablespoons oil
2 medium onions, finely chopped
30 ml/2 tablespoons flour
20 ml/1½ tablespoons cider vinegar
225 g/½ lb garlic sausage, diced

1. Put the lentils in a saucepan with the boiling water, bacon, vegetables and salt. Bring back to the boil, then simmer for 45 minutes.

2. Meanwhile, heat the oil in a frying pan. Add the onions and fry until softened. Sprinkle over the flour and stir in well. Cook for a further 3 minutes or until golden brown.

3. Remove the frying pan from the heat and stir in about 250 ml/8 fl oz of the soup until the mixture is thick and creamy. Stir in the vinegar, then add this mixture to the remaining soup. Stir well. Cover and simmer for 1 hour or until the lentils are tender.

4. Remove the bacon and cut it into dice. Return the bacon dice to the soup with the sausage, and salt and pepper to taste. Simmer for 5 minutes to heat the sausage.

Serves 6

Biersuppe
mit Schneebergen

(Beer soup with floating islands)

---

750 ml/1¼ pints brown ale
50 g/2 oz sugar
grated rind of 1 lemon
2 whole cloves
pinch of ground cinnamon
20 ml/4 teaspoons cornflour
2 eggs, separated
10 ml/2 teaspoons icing sugar

1. Preheat the oven to 220°C/425°F (Gas 7). Put the beer, sugar, a pinch of salt, lemon rind and spices in a flameproof casserole and bring slowly to the boil, stirring to dissolve the sugar. Dissolve the cornflour in a little of the beer, then add to the rest of the beer in the casserole. Simmer, stirring, for 3 minutes.

2. Remove the casserole from the heat and stir in the egg yolks. Whisk the egg whites until stiff. Add the icing sugar and whisk for a further 1 minute. Place spoonfuls of the egg white mixture on top of the beer soup.

3. Put the soup into the oven and cook for about 5 minutes or until the 'meringues' are lightly browned.

Serves 4

Markklosschensuppe

(Marrow dumpling soup)

---

150 g/5 oz fresh ox marrow
1 egg, separated
50 g/2 oz fresh breadcrumbs
25 g/1 oz chopped parsley
pinch of grated nutmeg
5 ml/1 teaspoon salt
900 ml/1½ pints beef stock or consommé

1. Crush the marrow and mix it with the egg yolk, breadcrumbs, parsley, nutmeg and salt. Whisk the egg white until stiff and fold into the mixture. Leave to stand for about 10 minutes.

2. Bring the stock or consommé to the boil in a saucepan. Form the marrow mixture into small dumplings using a teaspoon (dip it each time into hot water). Drop them into the stock or consommé and simmer until tender.

Serves 4

Bauernsuppe

(Peasant soup)

---

50 g/2 oz butter
1 kg/2 lb chuck steak, cut into small cubes
2 onions, chopped
25 g/1 oz flour
1 garlic clove, crushed
5 ml/1 teaspoon paprika
2.6 litres/4½ pints beef stock
1 bouquet garni
2 large potatoes, peeled and diced
7.5 ml/1½ teaspoons chopped fresh dill
50 g/2 oz grated Parmesan cheese

1. Melt the butter in a large saucepan. Add the steak cubes and brown on all sides. Add the onions and fry until softened. Stir in the flour, garlic, paprika, and salt and pepper to taste and cook gently for 5 minutes.

2. Gradually stir in the stock and bring to the boil. Add the bouquet garni. Cover and simmer for 1 hour, stirring occasionally.

3. Add the potatoes and stir well. Cover again and continue simmering for 45 minutes.

4. Discard the bouquet garni. Ladle the soup into individual bowls and sprinkle with the dill and cheese. Serve hot.

Serves 6

Bean Soup with Apples

450 g/1 lb French beans
350 g/12 oz potatoes, peeled and diced
1.7 litres/3 pints beef stock
1 bunch of summer savory
450 g/1 lb cooking apples, peeled, cored and sliced
125 g/4 oz streaky bacon, rinded and diced
1 onion, finely chopped
20 ml/4 teaspoons flour
10 ml/2 teaspoons vinegar
sugar

1. Remove the strings from the beans, if necessary, then cut them diagonally into small pieces. Put the beans in a saucepan with the potatoes and stock. Bring to the boil, then simmer for 45 minutes.

2. Add the summer savory and continue simmering for 5 minutes. Stir in the apples and simmer for a further 10 minutes.

3. Meanwhile, fry the bacon and onion together in a frying pan until they are lightly browned. Sprinkle over the flour and stir in well. Cook for 1 minute, then gradually stir in about 125 ml/4 fl oz of the stock from the saucepan.

4. Stir the bacon mixture into the soup in the saucepan. Add the vinegar with salt and sugar to taste. Simmer, stirring, until the soup has thickened, then serve.

Serves 6–8

Sahneheringe

(Herring salad)

---

8 large salted herring fillets, soaked in cold water for 24 hours
450 ml/¾ pint soured cream
1 large pickled gherkin, chopped
2 firm cooking apples, cored and chopped
2 onions, chopped
20 ml/4 teaspoons chopped chives
Marinade
45 ml/3 tablespoons vinegar
45 ml/3 tablespoons water
45 ml/3 tablespoons sugar

1. Drain the herring fillets and pat dry with paper towels.

2. Mix together the marinade ingredients in a shallow dish. Add the herring fillets and turn to coat with the marinade. Leave to marinate for a few hours, turning occasionally.

3. Drain the herring fillets and arrange them on a serving plate. Pour the soured cream over them, then sprinkle the gherkin, apples, onions and chives over the top. Serve with baked potatoes and beer.

Serves 6–8

NOTE: In Germany, this dish is usually made with salted herring fillets, which are not always available in the U.K. If you prefer to make the recipe with pickled herring fillets, remember to omit the marinade ingredients and step 2 of the recipe.

Wurstsalat

(Sausage salad)

---

450 g/1 lb mixed cooked German wurst, sliced
1 green pepper, cored, seeded and sliced
1 red pepper, cored, seeded and sliced
1 onion, thinly sliced into rings
2 small pickled gherkins, halved
Dressing
75 ml/5 tablespoons salad oil
30 ml/2 tablespoons vinegar
2.5 ml/½ teaspoon Dijon mustard

1. Arrange the wurst and peppers on a serving plate. Scatter over the onion rings and garnish with the gherkin halves.

2. Mix together the ingredients for the dressing and pour over the salad. Chill for 30 minutes before serving.

Serves 4

FISH

Gefullter Maifisch

(Stuffed Garfish)

---

4 garfish or mackerel, cleaned
30 ml/2 tablespoons flour
125 g/4 oz butter
Stuffing
90 g/3½ oz chopped cooked ham
4 tomatoes
4 slices of white bread, crusts removed
1 parsley sprig
125 ml/4 fl oz milk

1. Preheat the oven to 170°C/325°F (Gas 3). Rub the insides of the fish with salt.

2. To make the stuffing, mince together the ham, tomatoes, bread, and parsley, or purée in a food processor. Add salt to taste and the milk and mix well. Loosely stuff the fish with this mixture and sew up the openings.

3. Coat the fish with the flour. Melt the butter in a shallow flameproof casserole. Add the fish and brown on all sides. Transfer the casserole to the oven and cook for 30 minutes.

4. Serve hot with potato salad.

Serves 4

Perch Fillets
with Mustard Butter

1 kg/2 lb perch fillets, skinned
juice of 1 lemon
175 g/6 oz butter
1 onion, finely chopped
5 ml/1 teaspoon canned green peppercorns, drained and crushed
15 ml/1 tablespoon strong mustard
30 ml/2 tablespoons double cream
chopped parsley to garnish

1. Place the perch fillets on a plate and sprinkle with the lemon juice. Leave to soak for 10 minutes.

2. Pat the fish dry with paper towels, then season them with salt and pepper to taste. Melt 50 g/2 oz of the butter in a frying pan. Add the fish and fry for 5 minutes on each side or until cooked. Remove the fish from the pan and keep hot on a warmed serving platter.

3. Wipe out the pan with paper towels, then melt the rest of the butter in it. Add the onion and fry until softened. Stir in the peppercorns and mustard and cook for a further 2 minutes. Stir in the cream and pour this sauce over the fish. Sprinkle with chopped parsley and serve.

Serves 6

Katerfrühstück

(Pickled flounder)

---

700 g/1½ lb plaice or flounder fillets
juice of 1 lemon
50 g/2 oz butter
3 medium onions, sliced
2 large tomatoes, skinned, seeded and chopped
30 ml/2 tablespoons tomato purée
15 ml/1 tablespoon white wine vinegar
2.5 ml/½ teaspoon dried dill
3 pickled gherkins, thinly sliced

1. Put the fish fillets on a plate and sprinkle with the lemon juice and salt and pepper to taste. Leave to soak for 15 minutes. Preheat the oven to 190°C/375°F (Gas 5).

2. Meanwhile, melt 25 g/1 oz of the butter in a frying pan. Add the onions and tomatoes and cook until the onions are softened. Remove the pan from the heat.

3. Mix together the tomato purée, vinegar and dill in a small bowl.

4. Drain the fish fillets and arrange them, in one layer, in a greased shallow ovenproof dish. Spread the vinegar mixture over the fish, then pour over the onion mixture. Cover with the slices of gherkin. Cut the remaining butter into small pieces and dot these on top.

5. Bake for 15–20 minutes or until the fish flakes easily when tested with a fork. Serve hot.

Serves 6

MEAT

Gaisburger Marsch

(Beef stew with dumplings)

---

50 g/2 oz butter
700 g/1½ lb chuck steak, cubed
450 ml/¾ pint beef stock
5 ml/1 teaspoon vinegar
4 potatoes, peeled and cubed
45 ml/3 tablespoons oil
2 large onions, thinly sliced into rings
Dumplings
225 g/8 oz flour
5 ml/1 teaspoon salt
2 eggs, beaten
175 ml/6 fl oz milk

1. Melt the butter in a large saucepan. Add the beef cubes and brown. Stir in the stock, vinegar, and salt and pepper and bring to the boil. Cover and simmer for 30 minutes. Add the potatoes, simmer for 1 hour or until the beef is tender.

2. To make the dumplings, sift the flour and salt into a bowl. Beat in the eggs, then the milk. Leave to 'rest' for 10 minutes.

3. Drop 2.5 ml/½ teaspoonful of the batter, a few at a time, into a saucepan of boiling water and cook for 4 minutes or until soft. Drain on paper towels. Stir the dumplings into the stew and cook for 10 minutes.

4. Heat the oil in a frying pan and cook onions until golden. Drain on paper towels. Serve the stew topped with the onions.

Serves 4–6

Sauerbraten

1 × 1.6 kg/3½ lb topside of beef, boned and rolled
50 ml/2 fl oz cooking oil
2 medium onions, sliced
3 carrots, peeled and quartered lengthways
25 g/1 oz butter
25 g/1 oz flour
125 g/4 oz gingerbread or gingernuts, crumbled
50 g/2 oz slivered almonds
Marinade
600 ml/1 pint water
300 ml/½ pint red wine vinegar
300 ml/½ pint red wine
4 garlic cloves, halved
15 ml/1 tablespoon mustard seed
15 ml/1 tablespoon black peppercorns, crushed

1. Put the beef in a polythene bag and add all the marinade ingredients. Seal and refrigerate for 3 days. Remove the beef and dry. Strain the marinade and reserve.

2. Heat the oil in a large saucepan. Add the beef and brown on all sides. Add the onions, carrots, and 600 ml/1 pint of the marinade. Bring to the boil, then simmer for 2½ hours.

3. Transfer the beef and vegetables to a platter, slice and keep hot. Strain the cooking juices and measure them. If they do not make 600 ml/1 pint, add some of the remaining marinade.

4. Melt the butter in a saucepan. Stir in the flour and cook for 2 minutes. Gradually stir in the cooking juices and bring to the boil. Simmer until thickened. Stir in the gingerbread or gingernut crumbs and almonds. Cover and simmer gently for 10 minutes. Serve with the meat.

Serves 6

Boiled Beef
with Lemon Sauce

1 × 1.8 kg/4 lb topside of beef, boned and rolled
60 ml/4 tablespoons oil
6 black peppercorns
thinly pared rind of 1 small lemon
900 ml/1½ pints chicken stock
Sauce
75 g/3 oz butter
30 ml/2 tablespoons flour
45 ml/3 tablespoons lemon juice
125 g/¼ lb button mushrooms, quartered
1 egg yolk
30 ml/2 tablespoons soured cream

1. Rub the beef all over with salt. Heat the oil in a large saucepan. Add the beef and brown on all sides. Add the peppercorns, lemon rind and stock. Bring to the boil, then cover and cook gently for 2½ hours or until the beef is very tender. Remove the beef from the pan and keep hot. Strain the cooking liquid into a measuring jug. Skim off the fat and reserve 450 ml/¾ pint of the liquid.

2. Melt 25 g/1 oz of the butter in a saucepan. Stir in the flour and cook for 1 minute. Gradually stir in the reserved liquid. Bring to the boil and simmer until thick. Stir in the lemon juice and salt and pepper. Cook gently for 5 minutes.

3. Melt the remaining butter in a frying pan. Add the mushrooms and cook for 3 minutes, then stir into the sauce.

4. Beat the egg yolk and soured cream together. Add a little hot sauce, then stir into the rest in the pan. Cook gently until thick. Slice the beef and arrange on a platter. Pour over the sauce.

Serves 8

Rouladen

(Stuffed beef rolls)

---

6 slices of rump steak, about 15 × 20.5 cm/6 × 8 in
30 ml/6 teaspoons mustard
15 ml/1 tablespoon capers
15 ml/1 tablespoon sultanas
2 medium onions, finely chopped
40 g/2½ oz butter
4 carrots, peeled and finely chopped
3 tomatoes, skinned, seeded and chopped
5 ml/1 teaspoon sugar
425 ml/14 fl oz red wine
15 ml/1 tablespoon flour

1. Beat the beef slices with a rolling pin until very thin. Lay them out flat and spread over 5 ml/1 teaspoon of mustard. Sprinkle with the capers, sultanas and half the onion, then roll up and tie with thread.

2. Melt 50 g/2 oz of the butter in a large saucepan. Add the beef rolls and brown on all sides. Remove them from the pan. Add the remaining onion and carrots and fry until softened. Stir in the tomatoes and sugar, and cook for 5 minutes.

3. Stir in the wine and bring to the boil. Return the beef rolls, cover and simmer for 1 hour. Remove from the pan.

4. Strain the cooking liquid into a saucepan. Bring to the boil and boil for 15 minutes or until reduced by about one-third.

5. Mix the remaining butter with the flour to make a smooth paste. Add a little of the cooking liquid, then stir into the remaining liquid in the pan. Simmer, stirring, until smooth.

6. Return the beef rolls to the sauce and reheat for 5 minutes.

Serves 6

Pichelsteiner

(Meat and vegetable casserole)

---

60 ml/4 tablespoons oil
225 g/½ lb boned leg of lamb, cut into 2.5 cm/1 in cubes
225 g/½ lb boned loin of pork, cut into 2.5 cm/1 in cubes
225 g/½ lb chuck steak, cut into 1 cm/½ in cubes
225 g/½ lb pie veal, cut into 1 cm/½ in cubes
2 large carrots, peeled and sliced
½ small cabbage, trimmed and shredded
125 g/¼ lb French beans, sliced
4 celery sticks, sliced
1 medium turnip, peeled and chopped
2 leeks, white parts only, sliced
175 g/6 oz shelled fresh peas
1 large onion, chopped
2 large potatoes, peeled and diced
125 g/¼ lb ox marrow, chopped
450 ml/¾ pint beef stock

1. Heat the oil in a frying pan. Add the lamb cubes and brown on all sides. Remove from the pan. Brown the remaining meats in the same way. Mix together all the vegetables.

2. Cover the bottom of a large saucepan with the beef marrow. Make alternate layers of the meats and vegetable mixture on top, sprinkling each layer with salt and pepper. Pour in the stock. Cover the pan and simmer for 2 hours or until all the meats are tender. Serve hot.

Serves 4–6

Königsberger Klopse

(Meatballs in piquant sauce)

---

225 g/½ lb boned loin of pork, cubed
225 g/½ lb chuck steak, cubed
125 g/4 oz streaky bacon, rinded and chopped
2 onions, quartered
2 slices of white bread
5 ml/1 teaspoon chopped anchovy fillets
4 eggs
Sauce
50 g/2 oz butter
20 ml/4 teaspoons flour
50 ml/2 fl oz cream
2 egg yolks
10 ml/2 teaspoons vinegar
5 ml/1 teaspoon sugar
10 ml/2 teaspoons capers

1. Mince together the meats, onions, and bread, or use a food processor. Add the anchovies, eggs, and salt and pepper and mix together. Form the mixture into large meatballs.

2. Drop the meatballs into boiling salted water and simmer for 20 minutes or until just tender. Remove the meatballs with a slotted spoon and keep hot. Reserve 450 ml/¾ pint of the liquid.

3. Melt the butter in a clean saucepan. Stir in the flour and cook for 2 minutes. Gradually stir in the reserved cooking liquid. Bring to the boil, stirring, and simmer until thickened.

4. Beat the cream and egg yolks together. Add a little hot sauce, then stir into the rest of the sauce in the pan. Cook gently, stirring, until very thick. Stir in the vinegar, sugar, capers, and salt and pepper. Add the meatballs and reheat gently.

Serves 4

Berliner Eintopf

(Berlin stew)

---

40 g/1½ oz butter
1 large onion, chopped
3 potatoes, peeled and diced
225 g/½ lb French beans, chopped
2 carrots, peeled and diced
½ cabbage, trimmed and cut into 4 wedges
450 ml/¾ pint beef stock
15 ml/1 tablespoon tomato ketchup
5 ml/1 teaspoon mustard
15 g/½ oz fresh breadcrumbs
700 g/1½ lb cooked beef, veal or pork, cut into thin strips or diced
chopped parsley to garnish

1. Melt the butter in a large saucepan. Add the onion and fry until softened. Stir in the potatoes, beans, carrots and cabbage and fry for a further 2 minutes.

2. Add the stock, ketchup, mustard, and salt and pepper to taste and stir well. Cover and cook gently for 40 minutes.

3. Stir in the breadcrumbs and meat and cook for a further 5 minutes or until the stew is thick and the meat is heated through. Serve hot, sprinkled with parsley.

Serves 4

Hoppelpoppel

(Hash)

---

50 g/2 oz lard or butter
225 g/½ lb diced leftover roast beef or pork
225 g/½ lb diced cooked ham
225 g/½ lb diced sausages or frankfurters
450 g/1 lb potatoes, cooked in their skins, cooled and chopped
2 onions, finely chopped
4 eggs, beaten
chopped parsley to garnish

1. Melt the lard or butter in a large frying pan. Add the meats and potatoes and fry until all are lightly browned and piping hot. Stir in the onions, eggs, and salt and pepper to taste and continue cooking, stirring constantly, until the eggs are lightly scrambled.

2. Serve immediately, sprinkled with parsley.

Serves 4

Eisbein auf Sauerkraut

(Pickled pork with sauerkraut)

---

1 onion
4 salted hand and springs of pork, each weighing about 450 g/1 lb
5 coriander seeds
5 black peppercorns, coarsely crushed
20 ml/4 teaspoons salt
1 kg/2 lb canned sauerkraut, drained and roughly chopped
50 g/2 oz pork dripping
2 onions, finely chopped
300 ml/$\frac{1}{2}$ pint dry white wine
1 potato, peeled and grated
10 ml/2 teaspoons sugar

1. Cut the unpeeled onion in half. Heat a frying pan and brown the cut surfaces of the onion (this gives the gravy a better colour).

2. Put the pork in a large saucepan and add the onion, coriander seeds, peppercorns and salt. Cover with water and bring to the boil. Simmer for $1\frac{1}{2}$ hours.

3. When the pork has been cooking for 30 minutes, prepare the sauerkraut. Take 450 ml/$\frac{3}{4}$ pint of the pork cooking liquid and pour into another saucepan. Add the sauerkraut and bring to the boil.

4. Melt the dripping in the frying pan and add the chopped onions. Fry until golden brown, then add to the sauerkraut with the wine. Stir well and simmer for 40 minutes.

5. Stir the potato into the sauerkraut and simmer for a further 10 minutes. Add the sugar to take the edge of the sourness.

6. Arrange the pork and sauerkraut on a warmed serving platter and serve with potatoes.

Serves 4

Himmel und Erde

(Potatoes with apple and sausage)

---

1 kg/2 lb potatoes, peeled
1 kg/2 lb apples, peeled, cored and quartered
1 strip of lemon rind
20 ml/4 teaspoons sugar
125 g/4 oz streaky bacon, rinded and chopped
2 large onions, sliced
450 g/1 lb black pudding, sliced

1. Cook the potatoes in boiling salted water until tender.

2. Meanwhile, cook the apples in another saucepan with the lemon rind and sugar until soft and pulpy. Discard the lemon rind.

3. Drain the potatoes and return to the pan. Dry out over a very gentle heat, then mash well. Beat in the apples until smooth. Keep hot.

4. Fry the bacon in a frying pan until browned and crisp. Remove from the pan with a slotted spoon and stir into the potato mixture.

5. Add the onions to the frying pan and fry in the bacon fat until golden brown. Stir into the potato mixture, with salt and pepper to taste.

6. Pile the potato mixture on a warmed serving plate and top with slices of black pudding.

Serves 6–8

Loin of Pork
with Caraway Seed

75 g/3 oz butter
30 ml/2 tablespoons oil
1 × 1.4 kg/3 lb boned and rolled loin of pork
2 large onions, chopped
15 ml/1 tablespoon paprika
250 ml/8 fl oz dry white wine
150 ml/¼ pint chicken stock
30 ml/2 tablespoons flour
250 ml/8 fl oz soured cream
15 ml/1 tablespoon chopped chives
15 ml/1 tablespoon caraway seeds

1. Preheat the oven to 190°C/350°F (Gas 4). Melt 50 g/2 oz of the butter with the oil in a flameproof casserole. Add the pork and brown it on all sides. Remove the pork from the casserole.

2. Add the onions to the casserole and fry until golden brown. Stir in the paprika, wine and stock and bring to the boil. Return the pork to the casserole with salt and pepper to taste. Cover and transfer to the oven. Braise for about 1½ hours or until the pork is cooked through and tender.

3. Place the pork on a warmed serving platter and keep hot. Strain the cooking juices into a saucepan. Bring to the boil and boil until reduced by about one-quarter.

4. Mix the remaining butter with the flour to make a paste. Add a little of the cooking juices, then stir this mixture into the remaining juices in the pan. Simmer, stirring, until smooth and thickened. Stir in the soured cream, chives and caraway seeds and heat gently. Serve this sauce with the pork.

Serves 4–6

Labskaus

(Corned beef hash)

---

25 g/1 oz butter
2 large onions, finely chopped
450 g/1 lb corned beef, finely chopped
2 pickled herrings or rollmops, drained and finely chopped
1 anchovy fillet, finely chopped
6 large potatoes, peeled, cooked and mashed
5 ml/1 teaspoon lemon juice

1. Melt the butter in a frying pan. Add the onions and fry until softened. Stir in the remaining ingredients with pepper to taste and cook for 5 minutes, stirring occasionally.

2. Serve hot topped with poached or fried eggs.

Serves 4

(Top) Loin of Pork with Caraway Seed
(Bottom) Labskaus

Kasseler Rippchen

(Smoked pork chops)

---

25 g/1 oz butter
2 medium onions, chopped
2 medium carrots, peeled and sliced
2 large tomatoes, skinned, peeled and chopped
6 large pork chops, preferably smoked or cured
3 juniper berries, crushed
450 ml/¾ pint + 15ml/1 tablespoon cold water
10 ml/2 teaspoons cornflour
250 ml/8 fl oz soured cream

1. Preheat the oven to 190°C/375°F (Gas 5). Melt the butter in a flameproof casserole. Add the onions and carrots and fry until the onions are softened. Stir in the tomatoes and cook for a further 3 minutes.

2. Remove the casserole from the heat. Place the pork chops on top of the vegetables and sprinkle over the juniper berries. Add the 450 ml/¾ pint of water with salt and pepper to taste. Cover tightly and place in the oven. Cook for 30 minutes.

3. Reduce the oven temperature to 180°C/350°F (Gas 4) and uncover the casserole. Continue cooking for 40 minutes or until the chops are cooked through and browned. Transfer to a warmed serving platter, arranging the chops down the centre slightly overlapping. Keep hot.

4. Strain the cooking liquid into a saucepan, pressing down on the vegetables in the sieve with a wooden spoon. Bring to the boil. Dissolve the cornflour in the remaining water and add to the pan. Simmer, stirring, until thickened. Stir in the soured cream, then pour this sauce over the chops.

Serves 6

Falscher Hase

(Mock hare)

---

225 g/¼ lb chuck steak, cubed
450 g/1 lb boned shoulder of pork, cubed
2 juniper berries
5 ml/1 teaspoon dried marjoram
2 thick slices of bread
milk
1 leek, chopped
2 onions, chopped
225 g/½ lb pork sausagemeat
4 eggs, beaten

1. Preheat the oven to 180°C/350°F (Gas 4).

2. Mix the beef and pork with the juniper berries and marjoram. Moisten the bread with a little milk. Pass the meats, bread, leek and onions twice through the mincer, or use a food processor. Add the sausagemeat, eggs and salt to taste and mix together thoroughly.

3. Shape the mixture into a long roll with damp hands and place on a greased baking sheet. Alternatively, press the mixture into a loaf tin and place in a roasting tin containing hot water.

4. Bake for 1–1½ hours or until the loaf is golden brown.

Serves 4

German Country Supper

4 bacon rashers, rinded and chopped
1 medium onion, thinly sliced into rings
175 g/6 oz German sausage, such as Fleischwurst, chopped
4 small potatoes, peeled, parboiled, and sliced
25 g/1 oz butter
4 eggs
45 ml/3 tablespoons grated Cheddar cheese
chopped chives to garnish

1. Fry the bacon in a frying pan until it is crisp and has rendered its fat. Add the onion, sausage, potatoes and butter and cook, stirring, until the vegetables are lightly browned and the mixture is piping hot.

2. Beat the eggs lightly with the cheese and salt and pepper to taste. Pour over the mixture in the pan and stir to incorporate them with the sausage and vegetables. Cook gently until the eggs are lightly scrambled.

3. Serve hot, sprinkled with chives.

Serves 2–3

Venison with Pepper Sauce

4 venison chops
60 ml/4 tablespoons oil
175 ml/6 fl oz soured cream
5 ml/1 teaspoon grated horseradish
Marinade
125 ml/4 fl oz dry white wine
50 ml/2 fl oz olive oil
1 onion, thinly sliced
1 garlic clove, crushed
12 black peppercorns
5 ml/1 teaspoon dried thyme

1. Mix together the marinade ingredients in a shallow dish. Add the chops and turn to coat well. Leave to marinate in the refrigerator for 24 hours, turning occasionally. Drain the chops, reserving the marinade. Pat dry with paper towels.

2. Heat the oil in a frying pan. Add the chops and brown on both sides. Pour in the reserved marinade and bring to the boil. Cover and simmer for 20 minutes or until the chops are tender. Remove the pan from the heat and leave the chops to cool in the marinade. Cover and leave to marinate for a further 24 hours.

3. Return the pan to the heat and bring to the boil. Simmer for 15 minutes.

4. Transfer the chops to a warmed serving platter and keep hot. Strain the cooking marinade into a saucepan. Stir in the soured cream and horseradish and heat through gently. Pour this sauce over the chops and serve.

Serves 4

Hasenpfeffer

(Hare or rabbit casseroled in wine and herb sauce)

---

8 bacon rashers, rinded
75 g/3 oz flour
2.5 ml/½ teaspoon dried thyme
1 × 2.3 kg/5 lb hare (or rabbit), cleaned and cut into portions
15 g/½ oz butter
1 onion, finely chopped
2 garlic cloves, crushed
2 spring onions, chopped
250 ml/8 fl oz dry red wine
175 ml/6 fl oz chicken stock
15 ml/1 tablespoon cranberry sauce
5 ml/1 teaspoon chopped parsley
1.25 ml/¼ teaspoon dried marjoram
grated rind of ½ lemon

1. Preheat the oven to 180°C/350°F (Gas 4). Fry the bacon in a frying pan until it is crisp. Remove the bacon from the pan and drain on paper towels. Crumble and set aside. Mix the flour with the thyme and salt and pepper and use to coat the hare pieces.

2. Add the butter to the bacon fat in the frying pan and heat it. Add the hare pieces and brown on all sides, then transfer them to a casserole. Add the onion and garlic to the frying pan and fry until softened. Stir in the spring onions and fry for 2 minutes. Transfer the vegetables to the casserole.

3. Pour all the fat from the frying pan. Pour in the wine and stock and bring to the boil, stirring. Stir in the cranberry sauce, herbs and lemon rind. Pour over the hare and scatter over the bacon.

4. Cover the casserole and place it in the oven. Cook for 2½ hours or until the hare is very tender.

Serves 4–6

Roast Goose with Apple and Nut Stuffing

50 g/2 oz butter
2 large onions, finely chopped
350 g/¾ lb pork sausagemeat
4 large cooking apples, peeled, cored and sliced
175 g/6 oz dried apricots, soaked overnight, drained and chopped
grated rind of 2 oranges
125 g/4 oz toasted chopped hazelnuts
125 g/4 oz fresh breadcrumbs
30 ml/2 tablespoons chopped chives
2.5 ml/½ teaspoon dried marjoram
1 × 4 kg/8½ lb goose
1 lemon, quartered

1. Preheat the oven to 220°C/425°F (Gas 7). Melt the butter in a large frying pan. Add the onions and fry until softened. Add the sausagemeat and continue frying until it is no longer pink.

2. Remove the pan from the heat. Add the apples, apricots, orange rind, nuts, breadcrumbs, chives, marjoram, and salt and pepper to taste and mix together thoroughly.

3. Rub the goose inside and out with the lemon quarters. Discard the lemon. Prick the goose all over with a fork, especially around the thighs. Rub inside and out with salt and pepper. Fill with the stuffing, then truss.

4. Place the goose, breast up, on a rack in a roasting tin. Roast for 20 minutes, then reduce the oven temperature to 190°C/375°F (Gas 5). Continue roasting for 2½ hours or until the goose is cooked: test by piercing the thigh with a skewer – the juices that run out should be clear.

Serves 6

SALADS &
VEGETABLES

Kartoffelsalat

(Potato salad)

---

450 g/1 lb potatoes, peeled and quartered
6 bacon rashers, rinded
1 small onion, finely chopped
30 ml/2 tablespoons wine vinegar or lemon juice
1.25 ml/¼ teaspoon mustard powder
5 ml/1 teaspoon caraway seeds

1. Cook the potatoes in boiling salted water until tender.

2. Meanwhile, fry the bacon in a frying pan until it is crisp and has rendered its fat. Drain the bacon on paper towels and crumble.

3. Add the onion to the bacon fat and fry until softened. Remove the onion from the pan with a slotted spoon and set aside.

4. Add the vinegar or lemon juice, mustard, caraway seeds, and salt and pepper to taste to the frying pan and mix well. Remove from the heat and keep hot.

5. Drain the potatoes and cut them into cubes. Put into a large salad bowl and add the crumbled bacon and onion. Pour over the hot dressing and toss together thoroughly. Serve hot or cold.

Serves 4

Kopfsalat mit Buttermilch

(Lettuce salad with buttermilk dressing)

---

1 round lettuce, shredded
2 small potatoes, peeled, cooked and diced
4 bacon rashers, rinded, fried until crisp and crumbled
4 small pickled gherkins, finely chopped
1 small onion, thinly sliced into rings
Dressing
175 ml/6 fl oz buttermilk
5 ml/1 teaspoon brown sugar
5 ml/1 teaspoon lemon juice

1. Put the lettuce, potatoes, bacon, gherkins and onion in a salad bowl.

2. Put all the dressing ingredients in a screwtop jar and shake until well combined.

3. Pour the dressing over the salad and toss well. Serve immediately.

Serves 4

(Previous page)
(Top) Roast Goose with Apple and Nut Stuffing
(Bottom) Kartoffelsalat

Zwiebelkuchen

(Onion tart)

---

175 g/6 oz flour
40 g/1½ oz butter
40 g/1½ oz lard
60–75 ml/4–5 tablespoons iced water
Filling
25 g/1 oz butter
3 medium onions, thinly sliced
2 eggs, beaten
175 ml/6 fl oz single cream
5 ml/1 teaspoon caraway seeds

1. Preheat the oven to 200°C/400°F (Gas 6). Sift the flour and a pinch of salt into a mixing bowl. Rub in the butter and lard until the mixture resembles breadcrumbs, then bind to a dough with the iced water.

2. Roll out the dough on a lightly floured surface and use to line a 23 cm/9 in tart or flan ring. Prick all over with a fork, then line with foil and half fill with dried beans or rice. Bake the case for 10 minutes. Remove the foil and beans or rice and continue baking for 5 minutes or until firm and golden brown. Remove from the oven and set aside. Reduce the temperature to 190°C/375°F (Gas 5).

3. For the filling, melt the butter in a frying pan. Add the onions and fry until softened. Remove from the heat.

4. Lightly beat the eggs with the cream, caraway seeds, and salt and pepper to taste. Stir in the onions. Pour the filling into the pastry case.

5. Bake the tart for 40 minutes or until the filling is risen and golden brown. Serve hot or cold.

Serves 4–6

Leipziger Allerlei

(Mixed vegetables in cream sauce)

---

1 small cauliflower, broken into florets
175 g/6 oz shelled peas
225 g/½ lb asparagus spears, cut into 2.5 cm/1 in pieces
175 g/6 oz French beans
4 small carrots, peeled and diced
4 small button mushrooms
Sauce
25 g/1 oz butter
30 ml/2 tablespoons flour
250 ml/8 fl oz milk
250 ml/8 fl oz double cream
5 ml/1 teaspoon dried chervil
5 ml/1 teaspoon lemon juice

1. Cook the cauliflower and peas in simmering water for about 10 minutes. Add the asparagus, beans and carrots and cook for a further 5 minutes. Add the mushrooms and cook for a final 5 minutes or until all the vegetables are just tender.

2. Meanwhile, for the sauce, melt the butter in a saucepan. Stir in the flour and cook for 1 minute. Gradually stir in the milk and cream and bring to the boil, stirring. Simmer until thickened. Stir in the chervil, lemon juice, and salt and pepper to taste.

3. Drain the vegetables and put into a warmed serving bowl. Pour over the sauce and fold gently together. Serve hot.

Serves 4

DESSERTS & CAKES

Apfelbettelmann

(Apple pudding)

---

75 g/3 oz seedless raisins
90 ml/6 tablespoons orange juice
grated rind of 1 small lemon
225 g/8 oz fresh breadcrumbs, made from pumpernickel bread
175 g/6 oz brown sugar
125 g/4 oz chopped almonds
5 ml/1 teaspoon ground allspice
90 g/3½ oz butter, melted
700 g/1½ lb cooking apples, peeled, cored and thinly sliced

1. Mix together the raisins, orange juice and lemon rind in a mixing bowl and leave to soak for 30 minutes. Preheat the oven to 180°C/350°F (Gas 4).

2. Add the breadcrumbs, sugar, almonds, spice, and 50 g/2 oz of the butter to the raisin mixture and combine well. Put about one-third of the breadcrumb mixture on the bottom of a buttered 1.2 litre/2¼ pint capacity ovenproof dish and cover with half the apple slices. Add another third of the bread-crumb mixture followed by the rest of the apples. Cover with the remaining breadcrumb mixture. Pour the remaining melted butter over the top.

3. Bake for 35 minutes and serve hot.

Serves 6

Berliner Pfannkuchen

(Plum doughnuts)

---

20 ml/4 teaspoons dry yeast
350 ml/12 fl oz lukewarm milk
125 g/4 oz sugar
700 g/1½ lb flour
2 eggs
1 egg yolk
grated rind of 1 lemon
few drops of vanilla flavouring
50 g/2 oz butter, melted
225 g/8 oz plum jam
oil for deep frying
sugar for sprinkling

1. Stir the yeast into a little of the milk and add 10 ml/2 teaspoons of the sugar. Leave in a warm place for about 20 minutes or until frothy.

2. Sift the flour and remaining sugar into a mixing bowl. Add the eggs and egg yolk, lemon rind, a pinch of salt, vanilla, melted butter, remaining milk, and the yeast mixture. Beat to a dough.

3. Place the dough on a floured surface and roll out to the thickness of a finger. Cut into 7.5 cm/3 in rounds. Put a little jam in the centre of half of the dough rounds and put the remaining rounds on top. Press the edges together to seal, with damp fingers.

4. Leave the doughnuts in a warm place to rise for 10 minutes.

5. Deep fry the doughnuts, in batches, until they are golden brown all over. Drain on paper towels and sprinkle with sugar while they are still warm.

Makes about 16

Schwarzbrotpudding

(Black bread pudding)

---

225 g/½ lb cranberries
5 ml/1 teaspoon lemon juice
3 eggs, separated
225 g/8 oz sugar
1 ml/¼ teaspoon vanilla essence
2.5 ml/½ teaspoon ground cinnamon
225 g/8 oz breadcrumbs, made from black bread
75 g/3 oz plain chocolate, grated
whipped cream to decorate

1. Preheat the oven to 180°C/350°F (Gas 4). Put the cranberries in a saucepan with the lemon juice and just enough water to cover the bottom of the pan. Stew gently until the cranberries are tender.

2. Meanwhile, beat the egg yolks, sugar, vanilla essence, and cinnamon together until pale and thick. Fold in the breadcrumbs. Whisk the egg whites until stiff and fold into the breadcrumb mixture.

3. Drain the cranberries. Spread half of them over the bottom of a buttered 1.2 litre/1¼ pint ovenproof dish. Cover with half the breadcrumb mixture and scatter over all the chocolate. Add the rest of the cranberries and finally the remaining breadcrumb mixture.

4. Cover the dish with foil and bake for 50 minutes. Cool the pudding, then decorate with whipped cream.

Serves 8

Frankfurter Kranz

(Buttercream layer cake)

---

275 g/10 oz flour
10 ml/2 teaspoons baking powder
225 g/8 oz butter
225 g/8 oz sugar
6 eggs, separated
5 ml/1 teaspoon finely grated lemon rind
45 ml/3 tablespoons rum
Buttercream
175 g/6 oz unsalted butter
800 g/1¾ lb icing sugar, sifted
15 ml/1 tablespoon vanilla flavouring
60 ml/4 tablespoons whipping cream

1. Preheat the oven to 150°C/300°F (Gas 2). Sift the flour and baking powder into a bowl. In another bowl, cream the butter with the sugar until light and fluffy. Beat the egg yolks into the creamed mixture, one at a time. Fold in the flour mixture and the lemon rind.

2. Whisk the egg whites until stiff and fold into the batter. Spoon into a buttered and floured 23 cm/9 in ring cake tin. Bake for 1–1¼ hours or until a skewer inserted into the centre of the cake comes out clean.

3. Meanwhile, make the buttercream. Cream the butter until soft, then gradually beat in the sugar and a pinch of salt. When the mixture is pale and fluffy, beat in the vanilla and cream.

4. Cool the cake on a wire rack, then slice into three layers. Sprinkle each layer with rum and sandwich back together with about half the buttercream. Spread the remaining buttercream over the top and sides of the assembled cake.

Serves 8

Schwarzwaldkuchen

(Black Forest cherry cake)

---

5 eggs
175 g/6 oz sugar
50 g/2 oz flour
50 g/2 oz cocoa powder
150 g/5 oz butter, melted
Syrup
125 g/4 oz sugar
250 ml/8 fl oz water
Filling
900 ml/1½ pints whipping cream
50 g/2 oz icing sugar
225 g/½ lb canned Morello cherries, drained and dried
chocolate curls to decorate

1. Preheat the oven to 180°C/350°F (Gas 4). Beat the eggs and sugar until fluffy. Sift over the flour and cocoa and fold in with the butter. Divide between 3 buttered 18 cm/7 in sandwich cake tins. Bake for 12–15 minutes or until a skewer inserted into the centre of each cake comes out clean. Cool in the tins for 10 minutes, then cool completely on a wire rack.

2. To make the syrup, dissolve the sugar in the water. Boil for 5 minutes. Cool for 20 minutes, then prick the surfaces of the cakes and pour over the syrup.

3. Whip the cream with the sugar until thick. Spread a layer of cream over one of the cakes and cover with the cherries. Place another cake on top and spread with cream. Put the third cake on top. Spread about two-thirds of the remaining cream over the sides. Decorate with chocolate curls. Pipe the remaining cream on to the top of the cake and decorate with maraschino cherries and more chocolate curls.

Serves 10

Apfelstrudel

275 g/10 oz flour
1 egg, beaten
250 ml/8 fl oz lukewarm water
25 g/1 oz butter, melted
Filling
1.4 kg/3 lb eating apples, peeled, cored and thinly sliced
175 g/6 oz seedless raisins
75 g/3 oz chopped almonds or walnuts
125 g/4 oz butter, melted
50 g/2 oz fresh breadcrumbs

1. Sift the flour and a pinch of salt into a bowl. Mix together the egg, water and melted butter and add to the flour. Mix to a firm dough. Place on a floured surface and knead until it is smooth and elastic. Cover and leave for 30 minutes.

2. Meanwhile, make the filling. Mix together the apples, raisins and nuts.

3. Spread out a large cloth on a table and sprinkle with flour. Place the dough on the cloth and roll out as thinly as possible. Lift and stretch the dough, pulling it until it is paper thin. Trim the edges so the sides are straight.

4. Preheat the oven to 230°C/450°F (Gas 8). Brush the dough with half the melted butter and sprinkle with almost all of the crumbs. Spoon the apple mixture in a long strip on to the dough. Lift the dough over the filling and roll it up. Tuck in the ends. Brush with the remaining butter and sprinkle over the rest of the crumbs.

5. Cut the roll into pieces to fit on to greased baking sheets. Place the pieces on the sheets, seam underneath. Bake for 10 minutes, then reduce the oven temperature to 200°C/400°F (Gas 6). Continue baking for 20 minutes or until crisp and golden.

Serves 24

Dampfnudeln

(Sweet dumplings)

7.5 ml/1½ teaspoons dry yeast
45 ml/3 tablespoons lukewarm water
30 ml/2 tablespoons sugar
275 g/10 oz flour
1.25 ml/¼ teaspoon salt
125 ml/4 fl oz lukewarm milk
25 g/1 oz butter, melted
Cooking liquid
25 g/1 oz butter
30 ml/2 tablespoons sugar
125 ml/4 fl oz milk

1. Stir the yeast into the water and add 2.5 ml/½ teaspoon of the sugar. Leave in a warm place for about 20 minutes or until frothy.

2. Sift the flour, salt and remaining sugar into a bowl. Add the milk, melted butter and yeast mixture and beat to a smooth dough. Knead the dough for about 5 minutes or until elastic. Leave in a warm place to rise for 1 hour or until doubled in bulk.

3. Punch down the dough, then divide it into 12 pieces. Shape into balls. Place the balls on a baking sheet and leave in a warm place to rise for 45 minutes–1 hour.

4. To prepare the cooking liquid, melt the butter in a wide, shallow saucepan and stir in the sugar and milk. Bring to the boil. Place the dumplings in the pan, side by side, cover tightly and simmer gently for 20 minutes or until the dumplings are tender and have absorbed all the liquid. Serve hot, with stewed fruit.

Serves 4–6

Marmeladen-Torte

23 cm/9 in flan case made from shortcrust pastry, baked blind and cooled
Filling
60 ml/4 tablespoons apricot or blackcurrant jam
300 ml/10 fl oz milk
thinly pared rind of 1 lemon
60 g/2 oz fresh breadcrumbs
60 g/2 oz butter
60 g/2 oz castor sugar
2 eggs, separated
1.25 ml/¼ teaspoon grated nutmeg

1. Preheat oven to cool 150°C/300°F (Gas Mark 2). Spread the jam thinly over the bottom of the flan case and set aside.

2. In a small saucepan, combine the milk and lemon rind. Place pan over moderate heat and bring to just below boiling point. Remove from heat and set aside. Remove and discard lemon rind.

3. Place the breadcrumbs in a small mixing bowl and pour the milk over them. Allow to soak for 5 minutes. In another bowl, cream the butter and half of the sugar with a wooden spoon. Mix in the egg yolks and nutmeg and beat well.

4. Combine the egg mixture with the milk and breadcrumbs and mix well. Pour the mixture into the flan case and bake for 45 minutes. Remove tart from oven. Increase oven temperature to fairly hot 190°C/375°F (Gas Mark 5).

5. In a large mixing bowl, beat egg whites until they form soft peaks. Gradually add the remaining sugar, beating constantly. Spoon meringue mixture over tart and bake for a further 10 minutes or until meringue is lightly browned. Cool before serving.

Serves 6–8

Lebkuchen

(Spice cake)

---

3 eggs
175 g/6 oz sugar
425 g/15 oz clear honey
125 g/4 oz finely chopped almonds
grated rind of ½ lemon
grated rind of ½ orange
50 g/2 oz chopped mixed peel
275 g/10 oz flour
5 ml/1 teaspoon baking powder
1.25 ml/¼ teaspoon ground cloves
2.5 ml/½ teaspoon ground cinnamon
pinch of grated nutmeg

1. Preheat the oven to 190°C/375°F (Gas 5). Beat the eggs and sugar together until pale and fluffy. Stir in the honey, almonds, lemon and orange rind, and chopped peel. Sift together the flour, baking powder and spices and fold into the honey mixture.

2. Pour into a greased 20.5 cm/8 in square cake tin. Bake for 40–45 minutes or until a skewer inserted into the centre of the cake comes out clean.

3. Cool on a wire rack.

Serves 16

Käsekuchen

(Cheesecake)

---

175 g/6 oz crushed digestive biscuits
75 g/3 oz butter, melted
125 g/4 oz sugar
5 ml/1 teaspoon ground cinnamon
2 eggs, beaten
1.25 ml/¼ teaspoon salt
grated rind and juice of ½ lemon
125 ml/4 fl oz single cream
225 g/8 oz cottage cheese
50 g/2 oz chopped mixed nuts

1. Preheat the oven to 180°C/350°F (Gas 4). Mix together the biscuit crumbs, melted butter, 30 ml/2 tablespoons of the sugar and the cinnamon. Reserve 30 ml/2 tablespoons of this mixture, then press the remainder over the base and sides of a greased 20.5 cm/8 in sandwich cake tin. Chill until set.

2. Beat the eggs with the salt, lemon rind and juice, cream, cottage cheese, and remaining sugar. Fold in half the nuts. Pour the cheese mixture into the crumb crust and sprinkle the remaining nuts and the reserved crumb mixture on top.

3. Bake for 35–45 minutes or until a skewer inserted into the centre of the cake comes out clean.

4. Turn off the oven, open the door and leave the cheesecake inside to cool for 10 minutes. Remove from the oven and cool to room temperature.

Serves 8

Bremerkuchen

(Bremen sweetbread)

---

25 g/1 oz dry yeast
125 ml/4 fl oz lukewarm water
125 g/4 oz sugar
600 ml/1 pint + 175 ml/6 fl oz milk
150 g/5 oz butter
1.4 kg/3 lb flour
5 ml/1 teaspoon salt
2.5 ml/½ teaspoon ground cardamom
grated rind of 3 lemons
225 g/8 oz seedless raisins
125 g/4 oz slivered almonds

1. Stir the yeast into the water with 2.5 ml/½ teaspoon of the sugar. Leave in a warm place for about 20 minutes or until frothy. Scald the milk. Add 125 g/4 oz of the butter and heat until it has melted. Remove from the heat and cool to lukewarm.

2. Sift the flour, remaining sugar, salt and cardamom into a bowl. Add the yeast and milk mixtures and the lemon rind, and mix to a dough. Knead for about 10 minutes or until smooth and elastic. Leave in a warm place to rise until doubled in bulk.

3. Punch down the dough. Add the raisins and half the almonds and work into the dough until they are evenly distributed. Cut into two pieces and shape into long loaves. Place on greased baking sheets. Cover and rise for 45 minutes.

4. Preheat the oven to 190°C/375°F (Gas 5). Press the remaining almonds into the tops of the loaves. Bake for 1 hour. Melt the remaining butter. Remove the loaves from the oven and brush the tops with the melted butter. Serve cool.

Makes 2 loaves

Stollen

15 g/¼ oz yeast
175 g/6 oz sugar
175 ml/6 fl oz milk
125 g/4 oz butter
450 g/1 lb flour
5 ml/1 teaspoon salt
2.5 ml/½ teaspoon ground cinnamon
2 eggs, beaten
175 g/6 oz chopped mixed peel
75 g/3 oz sultanas
50 g/2 oz chopped walnuts
Icing
25 g/1 oz butter, melted
225 g/8 oz icing sugar, sifted
30 ml/2 tablespoons water

1. Stir the yeast into a little lukewarm water with 2.5 ml/½ teaspoon of the sugar. Leave in a warm place for 20 minutes or until frothy. Scald the milk. Add the butter and heat until melted. Remove from the heat and cool to lukewarm.

2. Sift the flour, remaining sugar, salt, and spice into a bowl. Add the yeast and milk mixtures and the eggs and mix to a dough. Knead until elastic. Leave until doubled in bulk.

3. Punch down the dough. Add the peel, sultanas and nuts and work in until evenly distributed. Shape into an oval and place on a greased baking sheet. Leave for 45 minutes.

4. Preheat the oven to 200°C/400°F (Gas 6). Bake for 15 minutes, then reduce the oven temperature to 180°C/350°F (Gas 4). Continue baking for 30 minutes.

5. To make the icing, beat together all the ingredients until smooth. Spread over the top of the stollen.

Spritzgebäck

(Hazelnut biscuits)

---

225 g/½ lb butter
225 g/8 oz sugar
1 egg, beaten
5 ml/1 teaspoon vanilla flavouring
1.25 ml/¼ teaspoon grated nutmeg
275 g/10 oz flour
2.5 ml/½ teaspoon baking powder
50 g/2 oz ground hazelnuts
15 ml/1 tablespoon icing sugar

1. Preheat the oven to 180°C/350°F (Gas 4). Cream the butter with the sugar until light and fluffy. Beat in the egg, vanilla and nutmeg. Sift the flour with the baking powder, then fold into the creamed mixture with the nuts.

2. Spoon the mixture into a piping bag fitted with a 1 cm/½ in plain nozzle. Pipe the mixture in spirals on to baking sheets.

3. Bake for 10–15 minutes or until the biscuits are just firm to the touch and golden brown around the edges.

4. Cool on the baking sheets for 5 minutes, then cool completely on a wire rack. Sift the icing sugar over the biscuits before serving.

Makes about 40

HOME-STYLE COOKING

CONTENTS

SOUPS

Philadelphia Pepper Pot

1 veal knuckle, sawn into 3 pieces
1 bouquet garni
6 peppercorns
5.1 litres/9 pints + 30 ml/2 tablespoons water
450 g/1 lb dressed tripe, cut into 2.5 cm/1 in pieces
1 onion, chopped
2 large carrots, peeled and chopped
2 celery sticks, chopped
2.5 ml/½ teaspoon red pepper flakes
2 medium potatoes, peeled and diced
30 ml/2 tablespoons cornflour
15 g/½ oz butter

1. Put the veal knuckle, bouquet garni and peppercorns in a very large saucepan and pour over the 5.1 litres/9 pints of water. Bring to the boil, skimming off any scum from the surface, then cover and simmer for 2½ hours.

2. Lift out the veal pieces and place them on a chopping board. Remove the meat from the bones and cut the meat into cubes.

3. Strain the stock and return it to the pan. Add the tripe, onion, carrots, celery, red pepper flakes, and salt and pepper to taste. Bring to the boil, cover and simmer for 1 hour.

4. Stir in the potatoes and veal cubes and simmer for a further 30 minutes or until the potatoes are tender.

5. Dissolve the cornflour in the remaining water and add to the soup with the butter. Stir until thickened, then serve hot.

Serves 6–8

Yankee Bean Soup

50 ml/2 fl oz oil
2 large onions, chopped
2 garlic cloves, crushed
6 tomatoes, skinned and chopped
4 celery sticks, chopped
225 g/8 oz dried red kidney beans, soaked overnight and drained
225 g/8 oz dried black beans, soaked overnight and drained
5 ml/1 teaspoon sugar
15 ml/1 tablespoon lemon juice
10 ml/2 teaspoons dried thyme
2.3 litres/4 pints beef stock

1. Heat the oil in a large saucepan. Add the onions and garlic and fry until softened.

2. Add the remaining ingredients with salt and pepper to taste and stir well. Bring to the boil, then cover and simmer for 3 hours.

3. Taste and adjust the seasoning before serving.

Serves 6

Cajun Gumbo

225 g/8 oz cooked ham, in one piece
1 garlic clove, crushed
4 onions, chopped
350 g/12 oz okra, sliced
700 g/1½ lb peeled shrimps
700 g/1½ lb tomatoes, skinned and chopped
175 g/6 oz tomato purée
750 ml/1¼ pints chicken stock
Tabasco sauce
1 green pepper, cored, seeded and chopped
450 g/1 lb cooked crabmeat, flaked
grated rind of 1 lemon
18 clams or mussels

1. Trim the fat from the ham and reserve. Cut the meat into cubes. Render the ham fat in a saucepan and pour off all but 30 ml/2 tablespoons. Reserve the remaining fat.

2. Add the garlic, onions, and okra to the pan and fry for 10 minutes. Stir in the shrimps and cook for a further 5 minutes. Remove the shrimps and okra from the pan and set aside.

3. Add the tomatoes to the pan with the tomato purée, stock, and several dashes of Tabasco sauce. Bring to the boil and simmer for 1½ hours. Stir in the ham cubes and okra and continue simmering for 30 minutes.

4. Heat the reserved ham fat in a frying pan. Add the green pepper and crabmeat and fry for 10 minutes, stirring frequently. Add to the tomato mixture in the saucepan, with the lemon rind and shrimps. Stir well.

5. Place the clams or mussels on top of the gumbo. Cover the pan tightly and steam until they open. Serve hot.

Serves 6–8

Manhattan Clam Chowder

125 g/4 oz diced salt pork
1 onion, chopped
4 large tomatoes, skinned and chopped
3 medium potatoes, peeled and diced
2.5 ml/½ teaspoon dried thyme
175 ml/6 fl oz tomato juice
600 ml/1 pint water
400 g/14 oz canned clams

1. Fry the salt pork in a saucepan until it has rendered its fat and the dice resemble croûtons. Remove from the pan and drain on paper towels.

2. Add the onion to the pan and fry in the pork fat until softened. Stir in the tomatoes, potatoes, thyme, and salt and pepper to taste.

3. Add the tomato juice, water, and juice from the canned clams. Bring to the boil, then cover and simmer for 12–15 minutes or until the potatoes are tender.

4. Stir in the clams and salt pork dice. Simmer for a further 5 minutes and serve hot.

Serves 6

(Top) Manhattan Clam Chowder
(Bottom) Pennsylvania Dutch Chicken Corn Soup

Pennsylvania Dutch Chicken Corn Soup

45 ml/3 tablespoons oil
2 onions, sliced
4 celery sticks, chopped
1.7 litres/3 pints chicken stock
10 peppercorns
125 g/4 oz egg noodles
450 g/1 lb chopped cooked chicken meat
450 g/1 lb canned sweetcorn kernels, drained
2.5 ml/½ teaspoon dried sage
1.25 ml/¼ teaspoon powdered saffron

1. Heat the oil in a saucepan. Add the onions and fry until softened. Stir in the celery and fry for a further 3 minutes.

2. Add the stock and peppercorns. Bring to the boil and simmer for 20 minutes.

3. Stir in the remaining ingredients with salt and pepper to taste. Simmer for a further 15–20 minutes or until the noodles are tender. Serve hot.

Serves 4–6

SEAFOOD

Baked Shad with Cornbread Stuffing

2 shad or herring fillets (about 450 g/1 lb)
75 g/3 oz butter
30 ml/2 tablespoons finely chopped spring onions
30 ml/2 tablespoons chopped green pepper
225 g/½ lb finely chopped mushrooms
40 g/1½ oz crumbled cornbread
50 g/2 oz crumbled water biscuits
5 ml/1 teaspoon dried dill
125 ml/4 fl oz water

1. Preheat the oven to 190°C/375°F (Gas 5). Lay the fish fillets in a lightly greased shallow ovenproof dish.

2. Melt 50 g/2 oz of the butter in a frying pan. Add the spring onions, green pepper and mushrooms and fry for 5 minutes. Stir in the cornbread and biscuits with the dill, and salt and pepper to taste.

3. Spread the cornbread mixture over the fish fillets, then fold them lengthways and tie in three places. Dot with the remaining butter and sprinkle with salt and pepper.

4. Pour the water into the ovenproof dish and cover loosely with foil. Bake for 30 minutes.

5. Remove the strings, cut the fillets in half and serve hot, garnished with lemon wedges.

Serves 4

Shrimp Creole

30 ml/2 tablespoons olive oil
2 large onions, finely chopped
1 garlic clove, crushed
250 ml/8 fl oz dry white wine
450 g/1 lb canned tomatoes, drained and chopped
15 ml/1 tablespoon red wine vinegar
15 ml/1 tablespoon sugar
1 large green pepper, cored, seeded and chopped
1 large red pepper, cored, seeded and chopped
15 ml/1 tablespoon cornflour
50 ml/2 fl oz water
700 g/1½ lb peeled shrimps

1. Heat the oil in a large frying pan. Add the onions and garlic and fry until they are softened. Stir in the wine. Bring to the boil and simmer for 10 minutes.

2. Add the tomatoes, vinegar, sugar, and salt to taste and mix well. Continue simmering for 10 minutes.

3. Stir in the peppers and simmer for a further 10 minutes.

4. Dissolve the cornflour in the water and add to the pan. Simmer, stirring, until thickened.

5. Stir in the shrimps and simmer for a final 5 minutes. Serve hot.

Serves 4

Shrimp Newburg

25 g/1 oz butter
225 g/8 oz peeled shrimps
50 ml/2 fl oz Madeira or sherry
2 egg yolks
450 ml/¾ pint cream
cayenne pepper
hot cooked rice or buttered toast
chopped chives or parsley to garnish

1. Melt the butter in a saucepan. Add the shrimps and cook gently for 5 minutes.

2. Stir in the Madeira or sherry and cook for a further 2 minutes.

3. Lightly beat the egg yolks with the cream. Add to the pan with salt and cayenne pepper to taste and cook gently, stirring, until the mixture is thickened and creamy.

4. Pour over hot cooked rice or buttered toast and sprinkle with chives or parsley.

Serves 2

Crab Louis

250 ml/8 fl oz mayonnaise
50 ml/2 fl oz double cream
50 ml/2 fl oz chilli sauce
50 g/2 oz chopped green pepper
30 ml/2 tablespoons finely chopped chives or spring onions
30 ml/2 tablespoons chopped stoned green olives
lemon juice
1 large lettuce, shredded
450 g/1 lb flaked cooked crabmeat

1. Mix together the mayonnaise, cream, chilli sauce, green pepper, chives or spring onions, and olives. Add salt and lemon juice to taste. Chill this dressing.

2. Arrange beds of shredded lettuce on four serving plates and pile the crabmeat on top. Chill.

3. Top the crabmeat with the dressing and serve.

Serves 4

Jambalaya

3 bacon rashers, rinded
1 onion, chopped
2 celery sticks, chopped
400 g/14 oz long-grain rice
600 ml/1 pint chicken stock
1.25 ml/¼ teaspoon cayenne pepper
1 bay leaf
1 large green pepper, cored, seeded and chopped
450 g/1 lb canned tomatoes, chopped with their juice
125 g/4 oz chopped cooked ham
225 g/8 oz chopped cooked chicken meat
225 g/8 oz peeled shrimps
chopped parsley to garnish

1. Fry the bacon in a saucepan until it is crisp and has rendered its fat. Remove the bacon from the pan and drain on paper towels. Crumble the bacon and reserve.

2. Add the onion to the pan and fry in the fat until softened. Stir in the celery and rice and cook, stirring, for 3 minutes. Add the stock, cayenne pepper, bay leaf, and salt and pepper to taste. Bring to the boil, then cover and simmer for 10 minutes.

3. Stir in the green pepper and tomatoes. Cover again and continue simmering for 5 minutes.

4. Add the ham, chicken, shrimps and crumbled bacon and stir well. Simmer, covered, for a further 5 minutes or until the rice is tender.

5. Discard the bay leaf. Serve hot, sprinkled with parsley.

Serves 4–6

MEAT

London Broil

---

4 × 225 g/½ lb rump steaks
Marinade
50 ml/2 fl oz white wine vinegar
50 ml/2 fl oz oil
1 garlic clove, crushed
15 ml/1 tablespoon lemon juice
4 peppercorns, coarsely crushed
5 ml/1 teaspoon salt

1. Mix together the marinade ingredients in a shallow dish. Add the steaks and turn to coat with the marinade. Marinate for 2 hours at room temperature, turning the steaks occasionally.

2. Preheat the grill. Drain the steaks and place them on the grill rack. Grill for 6–8 minutes on each side, depending on how well done you like your steaks. Serve hot.

Serves 4

Meat Loaf

700 g/1½ lb minced beef
350 g/12 oz minced veal
350 g/12 oz minced pork
4 slices of white bread
300 ml/½ pint milk
3 eggs
45 ml/3 tablespoons finely chopped celery
2 onions, finely chopped
30 ml/2 tablespoons chopped parsley
1.25 ml/¼ teaspoon dried thyme
1.25 ml/¼ teaspoon dried marjoram
1.25/¼ teaspoon dried basil
3 bacon rashers, rinded
125 ml/4 fl oz boiling water
50 ml/2 fl oz dry vermouth

1. Preheat the oven to 190°C/375°F (Gas 5). Put all the meat in a large mixing bowl. Tear the bread into small pieces and soak in the milk.

2. Add the eggs to the meat with the celery, onions, parsley, dried herbs, pepper to taste, and bread and milk mixture. Combine the ingredients thoroughly, using your fingers.

3. Shape the mixture into a loaf and place it in a buttered loaf tin. Lay the bacon rashers on top. Bake for 45 minutes or until the surface begins to brown.

4. Pour the boiling water over the meat loaf and continue baking for 45 minutes, basting once or twice with the vermouth and any juices that rise in the tin.

5. Unmould the loaf on to a warmed serving platter and serve hot.

Serves 4–6 with leftovers

Hamburgers

1.5 kg/3 lb minced beef
50 g/2 oz fresh breadcrumbs
5 ml/1 teaspoon dried thyme
1 egg, beaten
6 large hamburger buns, split

1. Preheat the grill. Mix together the beef, breadcrumbs, thyme, salt and pepper to taste, and the egg, using your fingers to combine the ingredients thoroughly.

2. Divide the mixture into six portions and shape into burgers.

3. Arrange the hamburgers on the grill rack and cook for 5–10 minutes on each side, depending on how well done you like your hamburgers.

4. Slide a hamburger into each bun and serve with sliced tomatoes, lettuce leaves, onion rings, ketchup and relishes.

Serves 6

New England Boiled Dinner

1 × 1.8 kg/4 lb salt brisket of beef
1 onion
1 bouquet garni
15 ml/1 tablespoon brown sugar
8 carrots, peeled
8 medium potatoes, peeled and quartered
6 small (button) onions, skinned
1 small cabbage, trimmed and cut into wedges

1. Place the beef in a large saucepan and cover with cold water. Bring to the boil, skimming off any scum that rises to the surface. When the scum stops rising, add the onion, bouquet garni and sugar. Half-cover and simmer for 2 hours.

2. Discard the onion and bouquet garni. Add the carrots, potatoes and small onions. Continue simmering for 30 minutes. Add the cabbage wedges and simmer for a further 15 minutes or until all the vegetables and the meat are cooked through.

3. Remove the beef from the pan and carve it into slices. Arrange on a platter and surround with the drained vegetables.

Serves 6–8

Red flannel hash : Leftover New England boiled dinner can be made into this classic. Mix together 450 g/1 lb of cooked beef, 4 cubed cooked potatoes, 225 g/8 oz cubed cooked beetroot and a chopped onion. Stir in 175 ml/6 fl oz of double cream, parsley, 5 ml/1 teaspoon of Worcestershire sauce, cayenne pepper to taste. Melt butter in a large frying pan, add the mixture and spread out evenly in the pan. Cook gently for 10 minutes, pressing down occasionally until a crust has formed on the base. Turn over and cook for 10 minutes or until a crust has formed. Serves 4.

Yankee Pot Roast

1 × 3 kg/6 lb topside of beef, boned and rolled
600 ml/1 pint red wine
1 onion, thinly sliced into rings
4 garlic cloves, peeled
7.5 ml/1½ teaspoons dried basil
25 g/1 oz butter
450 g/1 lb canned tomatoes, drained
50 g/2 oz stoned black olives
15 ml/1 tablespoon cornflour
30 ml/2 tablespoons water

1. Put the meat in a polythene bag. Add the wine, onion, garlic, and basil. Seal the bag and marinate in the refrigerator for 6 hours, turning the bag over occasionally.

2. Preheat the oven to 180°C/350°F (Gas 4). Remove the meat from the bag, reserving the marinade. Pat the meat dry with paper towels.

3. Melt the butter in a flameproof casserole. Put in the meat and brown on all sides. Pour in the reserved marinade and bring to the boil. Add salt and pepper to taste. Cover and place in the oven. Cook for 2 hours.

4. Add the tomatoes and continue cooking, covered, for 1 hour or until the meat is tender. Remove the meat from the casserole and carve it into thick slices. Arrange on a warmed serving platter and keep hot.

5. Strain the cooking liquid into a saucepan. Add the olives and bring to the boil.

6. Dissolve the cornflour in the water and add to the pan. Simmer, stirring, until thickened. Pour the gravy over the meat and garnish with parsley.

Serves 10

Broiled Pork Chops

1 large onion, thinly sliced into rings
6 thick pork chops
Sauce
50 ml/2 fl oz red wine vinegar
125 ml/4 fl oz tomato ketchup
10 ml/2 teaspoons sugar
2.5 ml/½ teaspoon ground cloves
5 ml/1 teaspoon celery seed
2.5 ml/½ teaspoon mustard powder
1 bay leaf

1. Preheat the oven to 180°C/350°F (Gas 4). Spread the onion rings over the bottom of a greased shallow ovenproof dish that is large enough to hold the chops in one layer. Rub the chops with salt and pepper and place them in the dish.

2. Mix together all the ingredients for the sauce and pour over the chops.

3. Bake for 1 hour or until the chops are cooked through and tender. Discard the bay leaf before serving.

Serves 6

Baked Spareribs

25 g/1 oz bacon dripping or butter
1 onion, chopped
30 ml/2 tablespoons vinegar
30 ml/2 tablespoons sugar
50 ml/2 fl oz lemon juice
250 ml/8 fl oz tomato ketchup
45 ml/3 tablespoons Worcestershire sauce
10 ml/2 teaspoons strong mustard
125 ml/4 fl oz water
5 ml/1 teaspoon dried basil
15 ml/1 tablespoon chilli powder (optional)
30 ml/2 tablespoons chopped parsley
1.8 kg/4 lb American-cut pork spareribs

1. Preheat the oven to 230°C/450°F (Gas 8). Melt the bacon dripping or butter in a saucepan. Add the onion and fry until softened. Stir in the vinegar, sugar, lemon juice, ketchup, Worcestershire sauce, mustard, water, basil, chilli powder, if used, and parsley. Bring to the boil and simmer for 30 minutes.

2. Meanwhile, sprinkle the ribs with salt and pepper and arrange them on a rack in a roasting tin. Bake for 30 minutes. Drain the fat from the roasting tin. Remove the rack and place the ribs in the tin. Brush them with the cooked sauce.

3. Reduce the oven temperature to 150°C/300°F (Gas 2) and bake the ribs for a further 1½ hours, brushing them frequently with the sauce.

Serves 4

CHICKEN

Creamed Chicken Livers

50 g/2 oz butter
2 onions, thinly sliced into rings
12 chicken livers, cut into strips
250 ml/8 fl oz cream
2 hard-boiled eggs, chopped
10 ml/2 teaspoons paprika
hot cooked rice

1. Melt half the butter in a frying pan. Add the onions and fry until golden brown. Remove the onions from the pan using a slotted spoon.

2. Add the chicken liver to the pan and fry for 5 minutes, stirring frequently. Remove the liver from the pan with a slotted spoon.

3. Add the remaining butter to the pan and melt it. Stir in the cream, eggs, paprika, and salt and pepper to taste. Return the liver and onions to the pan and mix into the sauce. Cook gently for 5 minutes.

4. Serve hot, with rice.

Serves 4

Chicken Maryland

25 g/1 oz flour
15 ml/1 tablespoon grated lemon rind
2 × 1 kg/2 lb chickens, halved
2 eggs, beaten
75 g/3 oz fresh breadcrumbs
oil for deep frying
50 g/2 oz butter
4 bananas, peeled and sliced lengthways
Corn fritters
125 g/4 oz flour
1 egg
175 ml/6 fl oz milk
225 g/8 oz sweetcorn kernels

1. Put the flour, lemon rind, and salt and pepper into a polythene bag. Add the chicken pieces and shake to coat them on all sides. Dip the chicken pieces in the beaten eggs, then coat with breadcrumbs. Repeat the egg-and-crumbing process, then chill the chicken for 2 hours.

2. Meanwhile, for the corn fritters, sift the flour and a little salt into a mixing bowl. Add the egg and milk and beat to make a smooth batter. Stir in the corn.

3. Heat oil in a deep fat fryer to 180°C/350°F. Deep fry the chicken pieces, two at a time, for 15–20 minutes. Drain on paper towels.

4. Increase the heat of the oil to 190°C/375°F. Drop heaped tablespoons of the corn batter into the oil and fry for 3 minutes or until puffed up and golden. Drain on paper towels and keep hot.

5. Melt the butter in a frying pan. Add the bananas and fry for about 3 minutes or until golden brown on both sides. Serve the chicken with the fritters and fried bananas.

Serves 4

Chicken Tetrazzini

175 g/6 oz vermicelli
65 g/2½ oz butter
30 ml/2 tablespoons flour
450 ml/¾ pint chicken stock
grated nutmeg
250 ml/8 fl oz double cream
45 ml/3 tablespoons pale dry sherry or white wine
700 g/1½ lb shredded cooked chicken meat
225 g/½ lb mushrooms, sliced
50 g/2 oz Parmesan cheese, grated

1. Preheat the grill. Cook the vermicelli in boiling water until it is tender. Drain and set aside.

2. Meanwhile, melt 50 g/1½ oz of the butter in a saucepan. Stir in the flour and cook for 3 minutes. Gradually stir in the stock. Bring to the boil, stirring, and simmer until thickened and smooth. Season with salt, pepper, and nutmeg. Stir in the cream, sherry or wine and chicken. Remove from the heat and keep hot.

3. Melt the remaining butter in a frying pan. Add the mushrooms and fry briskly until just tender.

4. Spread the vermicelli in a buttered flameproof dish. Scatter over the mushrooms. Pour the chicken mixture over the top.

5. Sprinkle with the cheese and grill just long enough to brown the top. Serve bubbling hot.

Serves 4

Chicken à la King

25 g/1 oz butter
1 green pepper, cored, seeded and finely chopped
175 g/6 oz thinly sliced mushrooms
15 ml/1 tablespoon flour
5 ml/1 teaspoon salt
350 ml/12 fl oz milk
250 ml/8 fl oz cream
700 g/1½ lb diced cooked chicken meat
3 egg yolks
10 ml/2 teaspoons lemon juice
15 ml/1 tablespoon paprika
10 ml/2 teaspoons chopped parsley
45 ml/3 tablespoons sweet sherry

1. Melt the butter in a saucepan. Add the green pepper and fry for 5 minutes. Add the mushrooms and continue frying for 3 minutes.

2. Stir in the flour and salt and cook for 2 minutes. Gradually stir in the milk and cream. Bring to the boil, stirring. Add the chicken and mix well. Cook very gently for 5 minutes.

3. Lightly beat the egg yolks with the lemon juice, paprika, parsley and sherry. Add about 60 ml/4 tablespoons of the hot sauce from the pan, then stir this mixture into the remaining sauce. Continue cooking very gently for about 4 minutes. Do not let the mixture boil. Serve hot, with rice.

Serves 4

Brunswick Stew

65 g/2¼ oz butter
8 chicken pieces
1 large onion, sliced
1 green pepper, cored, seeded and chopped
300 ml/½ pint chicken stock
450 g/1 lb canned tomatoes, drained
2.5 ml/½ teaspoon cayenne pepper
15 ml/1 tablespoon Worcestershire sauce
2.5 ml/½ teaspoon salt
225 g/8 oz canned sweetcorn kernels
450 g/1 lb canned butter beans
15 ml/1 tablespoon flour

1. Melt 50 g/2 oz of the butter in a large saucepan. Add the chicken pieces and brown on all sides. Remove the chicken from the pan.

2. Add the onion and green pepper to the pan and fry until the onion is softened. Stir in the stock, tomatoes, cayenne pepper, Worcestershire sauce and salt and bring to the boil. Return the chicken pieces to the pan. Cover and simmer for 40 minutes.

3. Stir in the sweetcorn and butter beans and continue simmering, covered, for 15 minutes.

4. Mix the remaining butter with the flour to make a paste. Add to the stew in small pieces and stir until thickened. Taste and adjust the seasoning before serving.

Serves 4–6

VEGETABLES
& SALADS

Succotash

4 bacon rashers, rinded
350 g/12 oz canned sweetcorn
350 g/12 oz canned butter beans
75 ml/3 fl oz cream

1. Fry the bacon in a saucepan until it has rendered its fat and is crisp. Drain on paper towels. Crumble and reserve.

2. Pour off all but about 20 ml/1½ tablespoons of the bacon fat from the pan. Add the sweetcorn and butter beans and heat through gently, stirring.

3. Stir in the cream, crumbled bacon, and salt and pepper to taste. Cook gently for a further 3 minutes or until piping hot.

Serves 4

Harvard Beets

450 g/1 lb beetroot
50 g/2 oz sugar
5 ml/1 teaspoon cornflour
50 ml/2 fl oz vinegar
125 ml/4 fl oz water

1. Put the beetroots into a saucepan and cover with water. Bring to the boil, cover and simmer for 50 minutes–1¼ hours, depending on the size of the beetroots. Drain and, when cool enough to handle, peel and slice.

2. Mix together the sugar and cornflour. Put the vinegar and water in a saucepan and heat until lukewarm. Stir in the sugar mixture and bring to the boil, stirring. Simmer for 2 minutes or until smooth and thick.

3. Add the beetroot to the pan and baste well with the sauce. Cook gently for 5 minutes or until the beetroot is heated through. Serve hot.

Serves 4

Boston Baked Beans

1 kg/2 lb dried haricot or kidney beans
10 ml/2 teaspoons salt
1 large onion, chopped
225 g/½ lb salt pork, thickly sliced
75 g/3 oz brown sugar
75 ml/5 tablespoons molasses
15 ml/1 tablespoon mustard powder
5 ml/1 teaspoon pepper

1. Put the beans in a saucepan and cover with cold water. Add half the salt. Bring to the boil, then half-cover the pan and simmer for 30 minutes.

2. Preheat the oven to 130°C/250°F (Gas ½). Drain the beans. Put the onion in the bottom of a casserole. Add a layer of beans, then cover with half the salt pork slices. Add the remaining beans and salt pork.

3. Mix together the sugar, molasses, mustard, pepper, and remaining salt. Pour into the casserole and add enough boiling water to cover the mixture.

4. Cover and bake for 5 hours, adding more boiling water from time to time so that the beans are kept covered.

5. Take off the lid and continue baking for 45 minutes or until a crust has formed on top. Serve hot.

Serves 6–8

Chef's Salad

1 lettuce, shredded
125 g/4 oz cooked chicken meat, cut into strips
125 g/4 oz cooked ham, cut into strips
125 g/4 oz Gruyère cheese, cut into strips
2 hard-boiled eggs, thinly sliced
15 ml/1 tablespoon finely chopped onion

1. Put the lettuce into a large salad bowl. Arrange the chicken, ham, cheese, and eggs on top and scatter over the onion.

2. Serve with your favourite dressing, such as French, Thousand Island or Blue Cheese (see page 296).

Serves 4

Caesar Salad

175 ml/6 fl oz olive oil
4 slices of white bread, crusts removed and cut into small cubes
1 garlic clove, halved
30 ml/2 tablespoons wine vinegar
5 ml/1 teaspoon lemon juice
2.5 ml/½ teaspoon Worcestershire sauce
1.25 ml/¼ teaspoon mustard powder
1.25 ml/¼ teaspoon sugar
1 egg
2 Cos lettuces, torn into pieces
6 anchovy fillets, chopped
50 g/2 oz Parmesan cheese, grated

1. Heat 50 ml/2 fl oz of the oil in a frying pan. Add the bread cubes and fry until golden brown on all sides. Drain these croûtons on paper towels.

2. Rub the cut surfaces of the garlic clove over the base and sides of a salad bowl. Discard the garlic.

3. Put the vinegar, lemon juice, Worcestershire sauce, mustard, sugar, the remaining oil, and salt and pepper to taste into the bowl. Mix well together.

4. Put the egg into a saucepan of boiling water and cook for 1 minute.

5. Meanwhile, add the lettuce to the salad bowl and toss to coat with the dressing. Scatter the anchovies, cheese and croûtons over the lettuce.

6. Break the egg on top. Toss the salad and serve immediately.

Serves 8

Blue Cheese Dressing

125 g/4 oz crumbled blue cheese
125 ml/4 fl oz mayonnaise
125 ml/4 fl oz double or soured cream

1. Beat the cheese into the mayonnaise, then beat in the cream.

2. Season to taste with salt and pepper and serve. Keep any leftover dressing in the refrigerator.

Makes about 300 ml/$\frac{1}{2}$ pint

Green Goddess Dressing

250 ml/8 fl oz mayonnaise
2 anchovy fillets, finely chopped
3 spring onions, finely chopped
30 ml/2 tablespoons chopped parsley
10 ml/2 teaspoons chopped fresh tarragon or 5 ml/1 teaspoon dried tarragon
15 ml/1 tablespoon tarragon vinegar
175 ml/6 fl oz soured cream

1. Mix together the mayonnaise, anchovies, spring onions, parsley, tarragon, vinegar, and pepper to taste.

2. Fold in the soured cream and chill for 30 minutes before serving. Keep any leftover dressing in the refrigerator.

Makes about 350 ml/12 fl oz

Mayonnaise, the basic ingredient in both Blue Cheese Dressing and Green Goddess Dressing.

DESSERTS

Maple Walnut Ice Cream

250 ml/8 fl oz maple syrup
3 eggs, separated
1.25 ml/¼ teaspoon salt
5 ml/1 teaspoon vanilla flavouring
250 ml/8 fl oz double cream
50 g/2 oz chopped walnuts

1. Put the maple syrup in the top of a double saucepan. Heat but do not let it boil.

2. Stir 30 ml/2 tablespoons of the warm syrup into the egg yolks, then add this mixture to the remaining syrup in the pan. Cook gently, stirring, until the mixture thickens.

3. Stir in the salt and vanilla and remove from the heat. Cool, then chill for 1 hour.

4. Whip the cream until thick and fold into the maple syrup mixture. Whisk the egg whites until stiff and fold in.

5. Remove the dividers from an ice cube tray and pour in the maple syrup mixture. Freeze for about 1 hour or until the mixture is frozen around the edges.

6. Tip the partially frozen mixture into a bowl and beat well. Stir in the nuts. Return the mixture to the ice cube tray and freeze for a further 3 hours.

Serves 4

Knickerbocker Glory

225 g/¼ lb strawberries, hulled and halved
4 scoops of vanilla ice cream
4 ripe peaches, peeled, stoned and sliced
4 scoops of chocolate ice cream
50 g/2 oz plain chocolate
45 ml/3 tablespoons brandy
175 ml/6 fl oz whipping cream
4 maraschino cherries

1. Divide the strawberries between four sundae glasses. Top each with a scoop of vanilla ice cream.

2. Divide the peach slices between the glasses and top with a scoop of chocolate ice cream.

3. Melt the chocolate gently with the brandy. Pour this sauce over the chocolate ice cream

4. Whip the cream until thick and pipe or spoon it over the chocolate sauce.

5. Top each sundae with a cherry and serve.

Serves 4

Cherries Jubilee

450 g/1 lb canned black cherries, stoned
1.25 ml/¼ teaspoon ground cinnamon
15 ml/1 tablespoon sugar
10 ml/2 teaspoons arrowroot
50 ml/2 fl oz brandy
vanilla ice cream

1. Drain the cherries, reserving 250 ml/8 fl oz of the syrup.

2. Put the syrup in a saucepan and add the cinnamon, sugar and arrowroot. Bring to the boil, stirring, and simmer until smooth and thickened.

3. Add the cherries and simmer for a further 2–3 minutes to heat them through.

4. Warm the brandy and add to the cherry mixture. Pour over vanilla ice cream and set alight. Serve flaming.

Serves 6

Strawberry Shortbread Cake

225 g/8 oz flour
50 g/2 oz icing sugar
175 g/6 oz butter
1 egg yolk
350 ml/2 fl oz double cream
450 g/1 lb strawberries, hulled
30 ml/2 tablespoons caster sugar

1. Sift the flour and icing sugar into a mixing bowl. Add the butter and cut into small pieces. Knead to make a smooth dough, adding the egg yolk and at least 30 ml/2 tablespoons of the cream. Chill for 30 minutes.

2. Preheat the oven to 190°C/375°F (Gas 5). Divide the dough in half and roll out each piece to a 23 cm/9 in round. Place the rounds on well-greased baking sheets. Mark one of the rounds into eight wedges. Bake for 12–15 minutes or until the edges of the shortbreads are golden brown. Cool.

3. Slice the strawberries. Whip the remaining cream until thick and fold in the strawberries.

4. Place the unmarked shortbread round on a serving plate and pile the strawberry and cream mixture on top.

5. Break the second shortbread round into the marked wedges and arrange these over the cream filling. Sprinkle over the caster sugar and serve.

Serves 8

Shoofly Pie

shortcrust pastry made with 175 g/6 oz flour
175 g/6 oz flour
125 g/4 oz butter
225 g/8 oz brown sugar
5 ml/1 teaspoon bicarbonate of soda
250 ml/8 fl oz boiling water
175 ml/6 fl oz molasses
175 ml/6 fl oz clear honey

1. Preheat the oven to 190°C/375°F (Gas 5). Roll out the dough and use to line a 23 cm/9 in pie dish or flan ring.

2. Sift the flour into a mixing bowl. Rub in the butter until the mixture resembles breadcrumbs. Stir in the sugar.

3. Dissolve the bicarbonate of soda in the water, then stir in the molasses and honey. Pour the mixture into the pastry case. Sprinkle the flour and butter mixture over the top.

4. Bake for 10 minutes, then reduce the oven temperature to 180°C/350°F (Gas 4). Continue baking for 25–30 minutes. Cool before serving.

Serves 4–6

Pecan Pie

shortcrust pastry made with 175 g/6 oz flour
50 g/2 oz pecans
3 eggs
250 ml/8 oz golden syrup
75 g/3 oz brown sugar
2.5 ml/½ teaspoon vanilla flavouring
1.25 ml/¼ teaspoon salt

1. Preheat the oven to 220°C/425°F (Gas 7). Roll out the dough and use to line a 23 cm/9 in pie dish or flan ring. Bake blind for 20 minutes or until golden brown and firm. Remove from the oven and cool slightly.

2. Arrange the pecans in the base of the pastry case in concentric circles.

3. Beat the eggs with the syrup, sugar, vanilla and salt. Pour over the pecans in the pastry case, being careful not to disturb their pattern. They will rise to the surface.

4. Bake for 10 minutes, then reduce the oven temperature to 180°C/350°F (Gas 4). Continue baking for 30 minutes. Cool before serving.

Serves 4–6

Coconut Cream Pie

shortcrust pastry made with 175 g/6 oz flour
225 g/8 oz sugar
65 g/2½ oz flour
750 ml/1¼ pints lukewarm milk
3 egg yolks
25 g/1 oz butter
5 ml/1 teaspoon vanilla flavouring
50 g/2 oz desiccated coconut

1. Preheat the oven to 220°C/425°F (Gas 7). Roll out the dough and use to line a 23 cm/9 in pie dish or flan ring. Bake blind for 20 minutes or until golden brown and firm. Remove from the oven and cool slightly.

2. Put the sugar and flour in a saucepan and gradually stir in the milk. Cook, stirring, for 10 minutes or until thickened. Cool slightly.

3. Beat the egg yolks with 45 ml/3 tablespoons of the milk mixture. Stir this into the remaining mixture in the pan. Return to the heat and cook gently, stirring, until the mixture is very thick. Stir in the butter, vanilla, and all but 30 ml/2 tablespoons of the coconut.

4. Pour the coconut mixture into the pastry case and sprinkle the reserved coconut on top.

5. Bake for 15 minutes. Cool before serving.

Serves 8

Chocolate Chiffon Pie

125 g/4 oz Brazil nuts
25 g/1 oz sugar
Filling
15 g/½ oz gelatine
125 g/4 oz sugar
1.25 ml/¼ teaspoon salt
250 ml/8 fl oz milk
2 eggs, separated
225 g/8 oz plain chocolate, broken into pieces
5 ml/1 teaspoon vanilla flavouring
350 ml/12 fl oz whipping cream
30 ml/2 tablespoons chopped Brazil nuts

1. Preheat the oven to 200°C/400°F (Gas 6). Grind the nuts in a food mill or blender. Mix with the sugar, then press over the base and sides of a 23 cm/9 in pie dish or flan ring. Bake the nut crust for 8–10 minutes or until lightly browned. Cool.

2. For the filling, put the gelatine, half the sugar, and the salt in the top of a double saucepan. Stir in the milk, egg yolks, and chocolate. Cook, stirring, until the gelatine has dissolved and the chocolate has melted. Remove from the heat and stir in the vanilla. Cool the chocolate mixture, then chill until it is on the point of setting.

3. Whip the cream until thick. Fold about two-thirds of the cream into the chocolate mixture. Whisk the egg whites until stiff. Add the remaining sugar and whisk for a further 1 minute. Fold the egg whites into the chocolate mixture. Pour the filling into the nut crust. Chill for 3 hours or until set.

4. Decorate with the remaining whipped cream and the chopped Brazil nuts.

Serves 6–8

Angel Cake

75 g/3 oz flour
15 ml/1 tablespoon cornflour
2.5 ml/½ teaspoon ground cinnamon
225 g/8 oz sugar
10 egg whites
15 ml/1 tablespoon lemon juice
15 ml/1 tablespoon hot water
5 ml/1 teaspoon cream of tartar
grated rind of 2 oranges
225 g/½ lb strawberries, hulled
icing sugar

1. Preheat the oven to 180°C/350°F (Gas 4). Sift the flour, cornflour, a little salt, and cinnamon into a mixing bowl. Add about one-third of the sugar. Sift these ingredients twice more.

2. Divide the egg whites, lemon juice, and hot water between two large mixing bowls. Whisk the contents of one bowl until foamy, then add half the cream of tartar and continue whisking until the mixture will stand in stiff peaks. Whisk the contents of the second bowl in the same way, adding the remaining cream of tartar. Tip into the first mixture.

3. Sift in the remaining sugar and the orange rind and beat for 1 minute. Gently fold in the flour mixture. Spoon into a 22 cm/8½ in angel cake or ring tin that is 10 cm/4 in deep. Bake for 45 minutes or until the cake will spring back when lightly pressed.

4. Remove the cake from the oven and invert it over a bottle or some other tall object. Cool completely.

5. Remove the cake from the tin and place it on a serving plate. Fill the centre with the strawberries and sprinkle with icing sugar.

Serves 8

Devil's Food Cake

125 g/4 oz plain chocolate
250 ml/8 fl oz milk
175 g/6 oz brown sugar
1 egg yolk
2 eggs, separated
275 g/10 oz flour
1.25 ml/¼ teaspoon salt
5 ml/1 teaspoon bicarbonate of soda
125 g/ 4 oz butter
175 g/6 oz caster sugar
50 ml/2 fl oz water
5 ml/1 teaspoon vanilla flavouring
1 packet American fudge frosting mix

1. Preheat the oven to 180°C/350°F (Gas 4). Put the chocolate, milk, sugar and 1 egg yolk in the top of a double saucepan. Cook, stirring, until the chocolate melts and thickens slightly. Remove from the heat.

2. Sift the flour, salt and bicarbonate of soda into a mixing bowl. In another bowl, cream the butter with the caster sugar until the mixture is light and fluffy. Beat in the remaining egg yolks, then add the flour and water and mix to make a smooth batter. Stir in the vanilla and the chocolate mixture.

3. Beat the egg whites until stiff and fold them into the mixture. Divide the mixture between three greased and floured 20.5 cm/8 in sandwich cake tins. Bake for 25 minutes or until a skewer inserted into the centre of each cake comes out clean. Cool on a wire rack.

4. Make the frosting according to packet instructions. Sandwich the cake layers together with about three-quarters of the frosting. Use the remainder to cover the top and sides of the cake, swirling it into a decorative pattern.

Serves 8

BREADS & COOKIES

San Francisco Sourdough Bread

1.5 kg/3 lb strong white flour
30 ml/2 tablespoons sugar
20 ml/1½ tablespoons salt
900 ml/1½ pints water
30 ml/2 tablespoons oil
Starter
225 g/8 oz strong white flour
125 g/4 oz sugar
450 ml/¾ pint milk

1. First make the starter. Put all the ingredients into a screw-top jar and shake to form a smooth paste. Leave, covered, in a warm place for 1 week.

2. Sift the flour, sugar, and salt into a bowl. Add the starter, water and oil and mix to make a dough. Tip the dough on to a floured surface and knead for about 5 minutes or until the dough is smooth and elastic. Shape into a ball and place in a greased polythene bag. Leave to rise for 2 hours.

3. Preheat the oven to 190°C/375°F (Gas 5). Punch down the dough and knead it for a further 10 minutes. Divide it in half and shape each piece into a round, about 15 cm/6 in in diameter.

4. Put the rounds on greased baking sheets. Cut a deep cross in the top of each round. Bake for 1–1½ hours: it should sound hollow like a drum. Cool on a wire rack.

Makes 2 loaves

Parker House Rolls

15 g/½ oz dry yeast
75 g/3 oz sugar
10 ml/2 teaspoons lukewarm water
350 ml/12 fl oz milk
140 g/4½ oz butter
700 g/1½ lb flour
5 ml/1 teaspoon salt
1 egg, beaten

1. Mix the yeast with 2.5 ml/½ teaspoon of the sugar and the water. Leave in a warm place until the mixture is frothy. Scald the milk in a saucepan. Remove from the heat and add 75 g/ 3 oz of the butter. Stir until the butter has melted, then leave the mixture to cool to lukewarm.

2. Sift the flour, salt and remaining sugar into a mixing bowl. Add the yeast and milk mixtures and the egg and mix to a dough. Tip the dough on to a floured surface and knead for 10 minutes or until smooth and elastic. Shape the dough into a ball and place it in a greased polythene bag. Leave to rise for 2 hours.

3. Punch down the dough and knead it for a further 3 minutes. Roll it out to about 1 cm/½ in thick. Spread 25 g/1 oz of the remaining butter over the dough, then cut it into 7.5 cm/3 in rounds. Make a shallow cut in the centre of each round and fold into semi-circles, pressing the edges together to seal.

4. Place the rolls on greased baking sheets, spacing them well apart. Melt the remaining butter and brush it over the rolls. Cover and let rise for 45 minutes.

5. Preheat the oven to 240°C/475°F (Gas 9). Bake the rolls for 15–20 minutes or until golden brown.

Makes about 40

Spoon Bread

150 g/5 oz maize flour
5 ml/1 teaspoon baking powder
1.25 ml/¼ teaspoon bicarbonate of soda
2.5 ml/½ teaspoon salt
3 eggs, beaten
450 ml/¾ pint buttermilk
25 g/1 oz butter

1. Preheat the oven to 200°C/400°F (Gas 6). Sift the maize flour, baking powder, bicarbonate of soda and salt into a mixing bowl. Add the eggs and mix well, then gradually beat in the buttermilk to make a smooth batter.

2. Put the butter in a 20.5 × 20.5 × 5 cm/8 × 8 × 2 in baking tin or a 1.3 litre/2¼ pint capacity soufflé dish. Warm in the oven until the butter has melted.

3. Remove the tin or dish from the oven and tilt it to coat the base and sides with melted butter. Pour any excess butter into the maize flour and stir it in, then pour the mixture into the tin or dish.

4. Bake for 35 minutes and serve hot.

Serves 4

Blueberry Muffins

400 g/14 oz flour
7.5 ml/1½ teaspoons salt
175 g/6 oz sugar
20 ml/4 teaspoons baking powder
4 eggs
125 g/4 oz butter, melted
300 ml/½ pint milk
275 g/10 oz blueberries or bilberries

1. Preheat the oven to 230°C/450°F (Gas 8). Sift the flour, salt, sugar and baking powder into a mixing bowl.

2. In another bowl, beat the eggs until they are pale and thick. Beat in the melted butter and milk followed by the flour mixture. Do not overbeat: the ingredients should be just combined.

3. Coat the blueberries or bilberries lightly in a little extra flour (this prevents them sinking to the bottom of the muffins), then fold them into the batter.

4. Divide the batter between 36 greased and floured muffin pans. Bake for 15 minutes or until risen and golden brown. Serve hot.

Makes 36

Brownies

---

175 g/6 oz plain chocolate
30 ml/2 tablespoons water
125 g/4 oz butter
125 g/4 oz sugar
5 ml/1 teaspoon vanilla flavouring
125 g/4 oz self-raising flour
2 eggs
50 g/2 oz chopped walnuts

1. Preheat the oven to 170°C/325°F (Gas 3). Put the chocolate, water and butter in a saucepan and heat gently, stirring until the mixture is smooth. Remove from the heat and stir in the sugar and vanilla. Cool slightly.

2. Sift the flour and a pinch of salt into a mixing bowl. Add the eggs and chocolate mixture and beat until smooth. Fold in the walnuts.

3. Pour into a greased 20.5 cm/8 in square baking tin. Bake for 30–35 minutes or until a skewer inserted into the centre comes out clean.

4. Cool in the tin, then cut into squares to serve.

Makes about 16

(Top) Brownies
(Bottom) Chocolate Chip Cookies

Chocolate Chip Cookies

---

125 g/4 oz butter
125 g/4 oz granulated sugar
75 g/3 oz brown sugar
1 egg
2.5 ml/½ teaspoon vanilla flavouring
175 g/6 oz flour
2.5 ml/½ teaspoon salt
2.5 ml/½ teaspoon bicarbonate of soda
50 g/2 oz chopped walnuts
50 g/2 oz chocolate chips

1. Preheat the oven to 190°C/375°F (Gas 5). Cream the butter with the sugars until the mixture is light and fluffy. Beat in the egg and vanilla.

2. Sift the flour with the salt and bicarbonate of soda, then add to the butter mixture. Beat until smooth. Mix in the walnuts and chocolate chips.

3. Drop teaspoons of the mixture on to greased baking sheets, spacing them well apart to allow for spreading. Bake for 10–15 minutes or until the cookies are golden brown. Cool on a wire rack.

Makes about 30

Pretzels

15 g/¼ oz dry yeast
2.5 ml/½ teaspoon sugar
250 ml/8 fl oz lukewarm milk
25 g/1 oz butter
350 g/12 oz flour
2.5 ml/½ teaspoon salt
15 ml/1 tablespoon caraway seeds
1 egg, beaten

1. Mix the yeast with the sugar and 30 ml/2 tablespoons of the milk. Leave in a warm place until frothy. Scald the remaining milk in a pan. Remove from the heat and add the butter. Stir until the butter has melted, then leave to cool to lukewarm.

2. Sift the flour and salt into a mixing bowl. Add 10 ml/2 teaspoons of the caraway seeds and the yeast and milk mixtures. Mix to a dough. Tip on to a floured surface and knead for 10 minutes or until smooth and elastic. Shape into a ball and place it in a greased polythene bag. Leave to rise for 45 minutes.

3. Punch down the dough and knead for a further 3 minutes. Roll into a sausage about 30.5 cm/12 in long. Cut the roll into 48 pieces. Roll each piece into a thin sausage about 15 cm/6 in long. Put on a flat surface and curve the ends towards you. Cross the loop halfway along each side and twist once. Bend the ends back and press firmly on to the curve of the loop.

4. Preheat the oven to 190°C/375°F (Gas 5). Drop the pretzels, a few at a time, into a pan of boiling water and cook until they rise to the surface. Remove and drain on paper towels. When all the pretzels have been 'boiled', arrange them on greased baking sheets.

5. Coat with beaten egg and the remaining caraway. Bake for 15 minutes or until golden brown. Cool on wire racks.

Makes 48

INDEX